LIPSTICK LASHES & GOD

ROSALES MAVERICKS
PUBLISHING STUDIO

Copyright © 2025, Gina Pero. All rights reserved. No part of this book may be reproduced, distributed, or transmitted in any form or by any means, including photocopying, recording, or other electronic or mechanical methods, without the prior written permission of the publisher, except in the case of brief quotations embodied in critical reviews and certain other noncommercial uses permitted by copyright law. V3

Title: Lipstick, Lashes, and God
Subtitle: Reviving the Spirit Within

Library of Congress Control Number: 2024906302

ISBN: 978-1-959471-46-2 (English Paperback)
ISBN: 978-1-959471-53-0 (e-Book)

Categories: Self-Help, Spirituality, Performing Arts

Cover design by: RMPStudio™
Team Editor: RMPStudio™ Team
Printed in the United States of America
Editor: Pam Zeidman, Kristen Dasto, Alison Kilian
Photographer: Cover Photo, McKenzi Taylor, Taylored Photo™

Order books: www.GinaPero.com

Publisher: Rosales Mavericks Publishing Studio™ (RMPStudio™)
1180 N. Town Center Suite #100, Las Vegas, Nevada 89144

Limit of Liability/Disclaimer of Warranty: While the publisher and author have used their best efforts in preparing this book, they make no representations or warranties concerning the accuracy or completeness of the contents of this book and specifically disclaim any implied warranties of merchantability or fitness for a purpose. All if any images are artificially created and do not represent any known persons. No warranty may be created or extended by sales representatives. Best Seller Disclosure on Amazon, Categories for Popular Dance, Performing Arts, and Prayer Books on the month of June 2025. This book is intended solely for informational and educational purposes and should not be construed as medical advice or used in lieu of professional medical expertise or treatment. The information contained in this book is not intended to diagnose, treat, cure, or prevent any disease. Readers are advised to consult their healthcare provider before following any of the advice or recommendations presented in this book.

To my Nana and Babci, my grandmothers who were faith made visible. Your living example became my divine teacher. Thank you for teaching me that the most beautiful dance is a life lived in harmony with divine grace and presence.

CONTENTS

Foreword 1

Introduction 5

    Part One: The Preparation 15

Divine Choreography 16

Curves of Courage 31

Angels in the Sky 49

The Sensitive Soul 71

Dialing Into Truth 87

    Part Two: The Performance 107

The Next Step 109

Divine GPS 127

The Divine Knockout 147

Starting Over 167

    Part Three: The Purpose 188

The Island of Remembering 189

Sacred Fire 211

Divine Surrender 237

Dancing with Divine Purpose 255

Afterword 267

Chapter Summaries with Reflective Questions 269

About the author 277

FOREWORD

There are moments in a father's life that become anchors in time, moments that flash before you with startling clarity no matter how many years pass. I remember the weight of my daughter Gina's tiny hand squeezing mine outside her kindergarten classroom, her eyes wide with a sensitivity to the world that I wouldn't fully understand for years to come. I remember the first time she stepped onto a stage how the shy little girl who once needed a chocolate chip cookie to enter a classroom suddenly embodied pure light in motion. I remember the day we learned about her scoliosis and how my instinct to protect her collided with her unwavering determination to dance.

Some of my most treasured memories are of Gina running into my arms after her performances, her face glowing with the pure joy that only comes from living one's truth. While her mother was the one making those countless forty-minute drives to David DeMarie Dance Studio, showing a dedication for which I'll forever be grateful, I had my own sacred moments with our daughter. In those quiet times when she curled up under my arm, seeking safety and comfort, I'd catch glimpses of the old soul behind her young eyes, and I'd know, with a father's intuition, that she was meant for something extraordinary.

When your child is born, no one hands you a manual for raising a highly sensitive, deeply spiritual being. You learn as you go, and sometimes, the greatest act of love is simply standing steady while they find their own way to bloom. Gina taught me this. While we thought we were supporting her dream of dance, she was actually teaching us about courage, about listening to the whispers of your soul, about finding strength in vulnerability.

Reading these pages, I'm struck by how the little girl who once couldn't let go of my hand has become a woman who helps others find their way back to themselves. The stories she shares here about transformation, about finding God in movement, about turning challenges into stepping stones resonate far beyond dance. They speak to anyone who has ever felt different, sensitive, or unsure of their place in the world.

As her father, I've had the privilege of watching Gina's journey from a front-row seat. I've witnessed her transforming physical limitations into spiritual strengths, converting her sensitivity into a superpower, and creating medicine from movement. But even I wasn't prepared for the depth of wisdom and raw honesty she brings to these pages.

Lipstick, Lashes, and God is more than my daughter's story; it's a testament to the power of listening to your inner voice, even when (perhaps, especially when) it leads you down unexpected paths. Through these pages, Gina invites you to discover what she learned in those early days at the dance studio: that our perceived limitations often hold the seeds of our greatest gifts, and that divine grace flows through every step of our journey, even the difficult ones.

As you read this book, I hope you'll feel what I've always felt watching Gina dance is that indescribable sense that you're witnessing something both deeply personal and universally true. These pages hold more than memories or lessons; they hold an invitation to discover your own divine choreography, to find your own way of dancing with life.

To my daughter: Your courage in sharing these stories makes me proud in ways words can't capture. You've always been my teacher as much as my child, showing me that true strength often comes wrapped in sensitivity and that sometimes the greatest act of faith is simply being exactly who you are.

To the reader: You hold in your hands not just a book but a permission slip to embrace your own sensitivity, trust your own path, and find the divine grace that flows through every step of your journey. Welcome to the dance.

With love and gratitude,

David Pero

INTRODUCTION

"How could You let this happen to me?"

These words, hurled at God from the floor of my teenage bedroom, where I lay alongside my plastic back brace, marked a pivotal moment in my spiritual journey. Not the polite prayers I'd been taught in Catholic school, but this raw, honest question born of pain, frustration, and a spine that curved like a question mark became the doorway to authentic spiritual connection. In that moment of angry questioning, I discovered something profound: genuine relationship with the divine begins not with perfect piety but with authentic truth. The space between my rage and surrender contained more sacredness than all my memorized prayers combined. It was the beginning of understanding that our most difficult moments aren't spiritual failures but invitations to deeper connection if we're brave enough to bring our whole selves, unfiltered and unpolished, to the conversation.

This realization would become the foundation for a lifelong journey of finding divine purpose not despite my challenges but through them, of discovering that our apparent limitations often contain our greatest gifts. It's a journey that would take me from a back-brace-wearing teenager to a Radio City Rockette, through an unconscious concussion and revelations, across oceans and into the deepest territories of surrender.

This book is an invitation to that same authenticity in your own spiritual journey, a path of honoring your unique design, recognizing divine guidance in unexpected places, and finding divine purpose in every aspect of your life, even the challenges.

The Divine Framework

Before we begin this journey, let me introduce you to the simple yet profound spiritual framework that emerged through my own path of discovery, what I've come to call "Lipstick, Lashes, and God." Far more than a catchy title, these three elements represent essential aspects of authentic spiritual living that, when integrated, create powerful transformation:

Lipstick represents courage, the willingness to be fully seen in your authentic truth. Just as applying lipstick makes your mouth visible, noticeable, impossible to ignore, spiritual courage means showing up without hiding your unique expression. It's about expressing your words intentionally, embodying your purpose fully, and sharing your diving gifts with confidence. Whether you wear actual lipstick or not, this principle invites you to fully express your gifts and shine with your own particular brilliance.

Lashes symbolize perspective, the lens through which you see yourself, others, and circumstances. Just as eyelashes frame your vision, your spiritual perspective frames how you interpret everything you experience. This element invites you to recognize beauty in unexpected places, wisdom in challenges, and divine guidance in unlikely messengers.

God embodies connection, your relationship with the divine presence in all things. However, you understand the divine, through traditional religion, nature, art, science, or personal spirituality, this element acknowledges that we are part of something larger than ourselves and that this divine presence also dwells within us. It invites you to recognize divine wisdom speaking through your body, your experiences, and your relationships. This connection isn't just reaching outward to something beyond; it invites us to also tune in to the sacred wisdom that has been within you all along.

When these three elements dance together, the courage to express your words intentionally, perspective to see divine guidance in all experiences, and connection to the divine presence, both within and around you, your becoming emerges naturally. You begin living as you were divinely designed to be.

Beyond the Name

Throughout history, across countless traditions, the divine has been known by over a thousand names: Yahweh, Allah, Brahman, Great Spirit, Divine Mother, Source, Universe, and Higher Power. Some traditions embrace 99 names, others 108, and still others refuse to name the divine at all, considering it beyond language's capacity to contain.

When you see "God" in these pages, know that I'm referring to that presence that transcends any single tradition or definition, the intelligence that curves a spine and then uses that very curve to teach wisdom, the love that sends a stranger with a prayer written on a napkin at precisely at the moment you need it, the mystery that weaves our challenges into our greatest gifts.

I was raised Catholic but have studied many spiritual paths, finding truth in each. The divine I speak of is not confined to churches or temples, holy books, or rigid doctrines. It's the sacred thread weaving through our everyday lives, present in both our struggles and our triumphs.

I use this particular word not to exclude anyone's understanding of the divine, but because it's the word that first formed on my lips when I asked my deepest questions. It's the language my soul speaks. Whatever name resonates with you, or even if no name feels quite right, I invite you to translate as needed, to hear beyond the word to the essence it points toward.

How to Use This Book

This book invites you to experience its wisdom through both reading and living. Each chapter introduces a spiritual principle illustrated through story and then provides practical ways to apply this wisdom in your daily life. As you engage with these teachings, I encourage you to:

Reflect deeply: Take time with the reminders after each chapter, allowing these insights to illuminate your own experiences and awaken your inner wisdom.

Apply intentionally: The three steps (Lipstick, Lashes, and God) offered in each chapter are invitations to embodied experience. Choose one that resonates and develop your own unique practice around it.

Integrate fully: Notice how the Lipstick, Lashes, and God elements align together in each teaching. Your true self emerges when you practice all three aspects as a unified approach to spiritual living.

Pray purposefully: Each chapter concludes with a prayer designed to deepen your connection within yourself and the divine presence. Use these prayers as you see fit, allowing them to become personal conversations that guide your journey.

Share authentically: Consider reading this book with others, creating space for shared reflection and accountability in applying these teachings.

Three Movements of the Spirit

This book unfolds in three parts, mirroring the divine choreography of a spiritual journey.

In **The Preparation**, we explore how physical challenges and emotional sensitivities become our greatest teachers. These foundational stories reveal how listening to your body's wisdom, finding courage in vulnerability, and recognizing the gift in sensitivity creates the essential groundwork for authentic purpose.

The Performance explores what happens when we step onto life's larger stages. You'll witness how a backstage concussion as Rockette, became a spiritual awakening, and how apparent setbacks often contain the seeds of our most authentic redirection. This section teaches discernment between worldly applause and soul-level resonance.

Finally, **The Purpose** reveals how true fulfillment emerges when we surrender control. From an Italian island where time slowed, to a Japanese temple where divine connection transcended religious structures, to the vulnerable dance of relationship, these chapters illuminate how removal from the familiar, unexpected spiritual encounters, and the courage to follow rather than lead ultimately reveal our authentic calling. Here you'll discover, the divine often works most powerfully when we finally release control.

Through all three movements, the Lipstick, Lashes, and God framework provides practical guidance for your own journey. Each chapter concludes with specific practices to help you apply these principles in your daily life, creating your own divine choreography.

The Journey Ahead

The chapters that follow invite you into a way of being that honors both your humanity and your divinity. They explore how the physical and the spiritual are not separate realms but interwoven aspects of the same divine dance.

Whether you're facing physical challenges, emotional hurdles, or spiritual questions, I invite you to receive these pages as a conversation between friends. My prayer is that these stories spark recognition of the divine choreography in your own life, illuminating the unique and purposeful dance you were created to perform.

With love and in movement,

Gina Pero

Part One: The Preparation

Where physical challenges and emotional sensitivities become our greatest teachers

"The experiences that stretch you beyond comfort, whether physical limitations, emotional sensitivities, painful setbacks, or unexpected words of belief aren't random challenges but divine choreography. Each movement, each position, each correction is preparing you for a dance you cannot yet envision but are perfectly designed to perform. " GP

DIVINE CHOREOGRAPHY

"Your body's signals are essential communications guiding you toward your next purpose step." GP

When the Body Reveals its Wisdom
Age 30-31 | New York City

The pulsing heartbeat of New York City echoed through my bones as I made my way through the crowded streets of Manhattan. Steam rose from the street vents, mixing with the early morning air, creating a mystical haze that seemed to dance alongside me. As a professional dancer in a city that never sleeps, I had grown accustomed to the symphony of taxi horns, street vendors, and the constant shuffle of people's dreams in motion. Yet beneath the exhilarating rhythm of my life as a performer, my body was telling a different story, one of imbalance, of scoliosis that curved my spine like a question mark, and legs that nature had crafted in slightly different lengths.

In the perfectionist world of professional dance, these physical challenges were more than mere inconveniences; they were potential career-enders. Every relevé, every grand jeté, carried with it a whispered prayer that my body would cooperate just one more time. That's when my friend introduced a Pilates instructor whose understanding of the human body seemed almost supernatural. During our sessions, her hands would hover over my misaligned shoulders, her voice gentle but assured. "Your body knows the way," she would say, "we just need to remind it how to listen."

It was the Pilates instructor who first mentioned Simonson Technique. A dance technique that emphasizes balanced alignment, deep stretching, proper muscle development, and natural range of motion through the joints. We were reflecting after a particularly challenging session, my muscles trembling from the effort to find balance. "Gina," she said, her eyes lighting up with that knowing look I'd come to trust, "you're ready for this" meaning I was ready to go experience a Simonson Technique class. We both knew my body was learning how to listen to its inner knowing and its own innate ability to warm-up efficiently. There was something in her voice, a mixture of excitement and certainty that made my heart skip a beat. I didn't question why; in New York, you learn to trust those moments of serendipity.

The following week, I found myself taking the subway downtown to the dance studio, my dance bag slung over my shoulder, nervous energy coursing through my veins. The studio space had extraordinary hardwood floors smoothed by countless feet, mirrors that had witnessed thousands of dreams being born and reborn, and windows that filtered the afternoon light into soft, golden streams. But as soon as the Simonson teacher began the class, I knew I had stumbled upon something miraculous. The tension that had been my constant companion, my silent partner in every performance, began to dissolve. Unlike the rigid, demanding techniques I had grown up with, this approach was different. The teacher's voice guided us through movements that felt like conversations with our own bodies. "Head to tail connection, and soften your sternum," she would say, and for the first time in my dance career, I wasn't fighting against my body's natural inclinations, I was flowing with them.

The transformation was profound. Each movement became a meditation; each stretch a revelation. By the end of that first class, tears were streaming down my face not from pain or frustration, but from an overwhelming sense of homecoming. Soon, these classes became the cornerstone of my week. Every Sunday and Monday, I would make my pilgrimage downtown, my heart lighter with each step. The studio became my church, the movement my prayer. Even the journey there became sacred: the way the afternoon light caught the buildings, the smell of fresh bagels from the corner deli, the nods of recognition from other dancers who shared this secret paradise.

Dance had always been my language, my way of speaking to the world. But now, through Simonson Technique, it was becoming my medicine. Even on days when my scoliosis screamed its presence, or my uneven legs made balance feel like a distant dream, I found joy in the movement of my body. My lower back pain began to slowly transform from an enemy into a teacher. For the first time I understood healing was possible. That was my brain emoji moment. The "Aha!" I couldn't believe there was a dance technique that could help me continue to love dance, now without pain and also help me learn how to love myself.

The universe has a way of placing the right people, places, and things in our paths at the perfect moment. One Monday afternoon, I was wrestling with whether to attend my Simonson Technique class. Despite my reluctance, there was this subtle but persistent inner voice urging me to go. Following this intuition would prove to be a pivotal decision. As I walked into the studio, I encountered a friend who asked, "Gina, are you going to do the Simonson Technique teacher training?" The question caught me off guard. I had been contemplating it but hadn't taken any concrete steps. "The application is due today," she added, "and Lynn Simonson herself is in the building." Learning that Lynn was in the building that very day felt like divine confirmation.

That small nudge that had brought me to class that day suddenly felt meaningful. Though I didn't get to meet Lynn Simonson after class as I'd hoped, that evening I went home and submitted my application. My fingers moved across the keyboard with certainty, each keystroke feeling like a step toward destiny.

Lynn's voice on the phone the next day carried the same assured gentleness I'd come to associate with the technique. "I need to share something with you," she began, her words wrapped in intuitive wisdom. "I interview every applicant personally. It's a gift I honor. And something is telling me this particular training, at this moment, isn't your path."

Instead of disappointment, I felt the strange lightness that comes with divine redirection. When I asked about alternatives, the conversation bloomed into something extraordinary. "I want you to audit the training," she said, her voice warming with possibility, "and then I'd like you to come to Seattle, to work with me one-on-one."

At that moment, I knew with absolute certainty that this was my path. Here was a woman who had never met me in person, yet she had recognized something in me that I hadn't yet recognized in myself. The series of events from the initial reluctance to attend class, to the timely encounter with my friend, to this unprecedented invitation felt like pieces of a puzzle falling into place perfectly.

This experience taught me the value of listening to those subtle inner promptings and remaining open to unexpected opportunities, even when they arise from what initially appears to be a "no." Sometimes, the universe has bigger plans than we can imagine for ourselves.

The flight to Seattle to learn with Lynn should have been straightforward, but life has a way of testing our resolve. I was sitting in an airplane seat, my body betraying me with an emotional reaction to the scent of a nearby cat and an anxious passenger. Panic began to rise in my chest like a tide, so I decided to walk to the back of the plane, where one aisle seat in the very last row was empty. Even in that moment of crisis, grace appeared in the form of a stranger the gentleman sitting across from me who, sensing my distress, wrote a prayer on a napkin and handed it to me. Those words became my mantra for the rest of the flight: "The light of God surrounds me. The love of God enfolds me. The power of God protects me. The presence of God watches over me. Wherever I am, God is."

Those words carried me through the flight and into Lynn's welcoming embrace. That first night in Seattle, as I drifted off into what Lynn had prescribed as necessary healing sleep, I felt a profound sense of peace. The next morning in Lynn's home, descending her stairs to find coffee and breakfast waiting, I realized this wasn't just about learning how to teach a dance technique, it was about coming home to myself. We started our training in her living room that afternoon, speaking about movement, yes, but also about life, about healing, about the incredible journey of becoming whole. Each day, we began our mornings with meditation and then allowed the lessons to reveal themselves as she taught me the first ten minutes of teaching a Simonson Technique class. Her gentle corrections of how I moved my body, a pattern I'd become accustomed to, was nourishing. Instead of forcing me to create a position with my body, she would guide my body to arrive in its shape with ease. Her approach was magical. How were her words able to direct my body to move so easily? How was my body so seamlessly able to change what it had done for so many years? Is this something I was going to be able to do for other dancers too?

I understood I was learning this technique for a higher purpose. Instead of needing all of the answers right now, I knew the "here" was most important. This quality time with Lynn was essential for my next life steps, and although I didn't know how the steps were going to show up, I knew deep inside that the universe's plan was arranging my path and for the first time I was okay with it.

Through learning one-on-one with Lynn, I discovered that sometimes our greatest challenges are actually invitations to deeper healing. My scoliosis and my uneven legs weren't obstacles to overcome, but teachers guiding me toward a more profound understanding of movement, of body wisdom, and ultimately, of myself. And then it hit me: This is exactly what I am going to be able to teach others how to do!

As I packed my bags after four transformative days with Lynn, I approached her with the question that had been weighing on my mind: "What should be my first step in beginning to teach the method?"

Her beautiful eyes met mine, filled with the innate wisdom that had guided so many before me. "I want you to put away all your notes and all your binders," she said. "When you walk into your first class, your students will lead you. Their bodies will speak to you, and you will know exactly how to start and where to finish. Trust in your students, Gina. Allow them to lead you. Allow yourself to know that you have an innate gift to see what the body requires and needs in each moment."

As I boarded the plane to return home to New York City, a sense of calm washed over me. I felt a renewed sense of spirit. Meeting Lynn was like meeting a living legend who turned out to be more wonderful than the legend itself. Her eyes held decades of dance wisdom, but it was her understanding of the human mind, the human body, and the human spirit that truly captured me.

This chapter of my life taught me that sometimes the most powerful prayer is simply saying "yes" to the unknown. In the gentle wisdom of Simonson Technique, I found not just a way of moving but a way of being. My body, with all its beautiful imperfections, wasn't something to be conquered, it was something to be listened to, honored, and loved. Your most profound teacher on the path to wholeness can be your body's wisdom when you simply listen, honor, and trust its natural design.

REVIVING YOUR SPIRIT

Reminders

Listen to your body's wisdom: Your physical challenges aren't punishments. They're pathways to deeper understanding. When you stop fighting your body and start listening to it, healing begins.

Trust divine timing: The aligned teachers, techniques, and transformative moments will appear when your spirit is ready. Stay open to unexpected guidance, even if it comes in the form of a stranger's prayer on an airplane napkin.

Listen to your body's signals: Spiritual revival begins when you honor both the "no" and "yes" responses from your body's innate wisdom. Trust your inner knowing when it recognizes a divine invitation for growth, even when your mind hasn't yet caught up with what your heart and body already know.

STEPS

🔹 **Lipstick:** Express, "My body is a sacred teacher." Place your hand gently on any area of tension and courageously ask what wisdom it has for you. This act of honoring your body's voice is your first step in expressing the authentic truth of your unique divine design.

🔹 **Lashes:** Shift your perspective. Notice the subtle intuitive whispers urging you toward or away from choices this week. View these bodily signals through the lens of divine wisdom rather than inconvenient interruptions. When your gut tightens or your heart expands in response to a possibility, see this as inner guidance illuminating your path with divine vision.

🔹 **God:** Connect with divine presence. Recognize how the divine speaks through your body's signals, through unexpected messengers, and through apparent redirections. Notice the surprising packaging these messages arrive in, like a stranger's prayer on a napkin, a "no" that can lead you to a greater invitation, or a physical limitation revealing greater purpose. Express gratitude for this divine choreography that flows through all aspects of your being.

PRAYER

Honoring Your Body's Wisdom

Divine Presence,

Help me listen to my body with reverence and respect. Teach me to hear wisdom in its whispers, guidance in its limitations, and purpose in its unique design. May I treat this vessel as a temple of divine intelligence.

When pain speaks, grant me courage to listen. When limitations arise, show me the gift within them. Transform my resistance into receptivity, my frustration into understanding, my judgment into compassion.

With each breath, remind me that this body exists as one with my spirit, the physical expression of my soul's journey. Help me honor its truth, trust its signals, and celebrate its divine choreography.

With ease, please, help me embrace the sacred wisdom dwelling within my own form.
Amen.

CURVES OF COURAGE

"What others might see as your flaws are actually your unique signature. Embrace your divine design that makes your contribution to this world unlike anyone else's." GP

Finding Grace in the Unexpected
Age 12-16 | Batavia and Buffalo, New York

Some gifts arrive wrapped in challenges, their true value revealed only through the patient unfolding of time and trust. At twelve years old, I stood in the gleaming halls of David DeMarie Dance Studio in Clarence, New York, the afternoon sunlight streaming through tall windows to create golden pathways across the polished floors. The familiar melody of piano music mingled with the percussive rhythm of tap shoes from the adjacent room, creating the soundtrack of my young dreams. I inhaled deeply, savoring the comforting blend of rosin dust, leather dance shoes, and the lingering notes of hairspray that signaled I was home one of Western New York's promising young dancers chosen for the studio's competition team.

Three or four times a week, the forty-minute drive from our home Batavia, NY, to the dance studio in Buffalo, NY, traced the geography of possibility. From my passenger seat window, I'd watch the landscape transform from small-town quaintness to suburban promise, each mile bringing me closer to becoming the dancer I yearned to be. My mother's hands on the steering wheel, slightly chapped from household work, the nails kept practically short but always clean, was a testament to her boundless love and unwavering belief in the gift she saw unfolding within me. The sacrifice of those drives painted evening highways with constellations of hope; at each headlight, we passed another star in the universe of my becoming.

One Tuesday evening would rewrite the choreography of my life in ways I couldn't yet comprehend. The studio mirrors, those unforgiving truth-tellers, reflected back rows of dancers executing combinations with the precision that our dance teacher demanded. Standing before them in my black dance team, leotard, black tights, and headscarf, the uniform that marked us as the dedicated, the chosen, I executed a simple relevé in first position, arms rising through preparatory to fifth position, when something caught my eye. An unusual indent on my right side, a subtle whisper of asymmetry that would soon crescendo into a life-changing revelation.

I walked toward the mirror, leaning closer while maintaining my turnout, shifting my weight to see more clearly. The hollow wasn't visible when I stood normally, but as I moved through positions, it appeared and disappeared like a shadow dancer partnering only with me. Questions pirouetted through my mind: Was this normal? Was I seeing things? Was I somehow different from everyone else in this room of perfection-seekers?

The drive home that night held a different weight, the car filled with the heaviness of unasked questions.

Streetlights created rhythmic patterns of light and dark across my mother's face as she navigated the familiar route home. Finally, during a long stretch of darkness between towns, I gathered my courage. I didn't want to burden my mom with worry or fear, so I hesitated until I couldn't hold in the words any longer.

"Mom," I ventured, my voice small against the hum of tires on asphalt, "I think there's something wrong with me." The words hung suspended in the car's interior, like dancers in mid-leap waiting for gravity's inevitable claim.

Her eyes found mine in the rearview mirror, filled with that mixture of strength and tenderness that only mothers possess. "Honey, I'm not sure I understand. What do you mean?" Her voice created a safe space for my fears to land.

My fingers traced the spot on my side, explanation flowing more easily through movement than words. "There's this dent in the right side of my body. I saw it in the mirror today during ballet. It's only on one side, not both." My mom, eyes on the road to conceal her worry, gripped the steering wheel as if she were putting her own fears into it and said, "Let's look at this when we get home or tomorrow when we can both pay attention." I sank in my car seat, looking out the window for the rest of the drive, knowing God was somewhere out there in the vast darkness, listening.

Divine timing works through the most ordinary circumstances. The very next day, during a routine scoliosis screening at my Catholic school, my gym teacher's expression shifted as I bent forward in what dancers know as "flat back." Her hands paused at my spine, fingers tracing the uneven ridges that had begun their silent rebellion against symmetry. "Gina, I think we need to have the school nurse take a look at this," she said, her voice carrying that measured tone adults use when trying not to alarm children.

My mother, who was the secretary at our grade school, appeared shortly after in the gym locker room, her worried eyes meeting mine across the space. The next day, we were on our way to a specialist in Rochester, another forty-minute drive together. The car ride filled us both with an anxiousness that felt like choreography we were both learning for the first time, slightly off-balance, searching for the rhythm of this new reality. Although I was unsure of the outcome, I was very sure that my mom would have a plan.

The orthopedic office smelled of antiseptic and old magazines. X-ray machines hummed and clicked as they captured images of my spine, the technician positioning me with clinical precision, so different from the artistic alignment I was used to in dance. When the films were developed, they painted the truth in stark relief: Scoliosis had curved my spine into a question mark, 17 degrees at the top, 36 at the bottom. The doctor's warning about surgery being necessary for curves over 40 degrees sent ripples of fear through our hearts.

"Will I still be able to dance?" The question burst from me before I could stop it, my priorities crystal clear even in that moment of diagnosis.

The doctor's eyes softened slightly, perhaps recognizing the dancer's soul beneath the medical concern. "For now, yes. But we need to fit you with a Boston brace to prevent the curve from progressing."

Before I could fully process this new reality, I found myself standing in a different sort of studio, a prosthetics lab, where experts in a different kind of body mechanics worked. The casting process felt like a cocoon of uncertainty being wrapped around not only my body but also my dreams. Technicians wrapped my torso in plaster, issuing careful instructions to "stay perfectly still," a cruel irony for a body trained to move. The sensation of the plaster warming against my skin, then being sawed down the middle to create a mold, created a soundscape of vulnerability I would never forget.

"Sixteen hours a day," came the sentence once my custom brace was ready, a rigid plastic shell lined with thin padding that imprisoned my torso from hips to armpits. "You can choose between wearing it during sleep or during dance classes, but the more you wear it, the more effective it will be."

The choice wasn't really a choice at all. Dance was my prayer, my connection to something greater than myself, my passion, and my dream. I would *never* choose to sacrifice dance, especially in this moment of need. The stage was where I felt most alive, most myself, most connected to the divine. If that meant sleeping in plastic armor, then that was the price I would pay.

The first weeks with the brace were a painful new choreography of learning how to sit, stand, and even breathe differently. The plastic edges dug into my hips when I sat too long; red marks and calluses formed at pressure points where bone met this stiff material. At night, lying in bed, I would trace my fingers along the smooth exterior of my medical armor, wondering if this foreign object would ever feel like part of me.

One night, after a particularly difficult day when a simple center combination had angered me because of my restricted movement, the accumulated weight of it all became too much to bear. The back brace, that rigid, uncompromising cage, flew across my bedroom in an arc of frustration, crashing against the closet door with a sound that echoed the storm inside me.

"How could you let this happen to me?" The question erupted from someplace deeper than my curved spine, challenging the God I'd been taught to trust unconditionally in Sunday school classes and family prayers. "I've done everything right. I've worked so hard." Tears flowed hot and fast, baptizing my pillow with disappointment.

My Catholic upbringing had given me prayers and rituals, but in that moment, I needed something more profound, something that could hold both my pain and my possibility. I needed a God who understood what it meant to have a body that refused to follow the rules. I was angry, and I was confused. What twelve-year-old girl deserved to go through this? What created this in the first place? I was asking for answers no, *demanding* them when a mysterious response appeared.

To my surprise, grace arrived in the form of an unexpected pilgrimage to Quebec with my grandmother and my aunt the following summer. My grandmother, who I called Babci, a woman whose faith was as practical as her perfectly set hair, had suggested the trip, and I was immediately on board. The bus ride, with its many rosaries, prayer, and quality time with people who were living by faith, caught my childhood attention. Why did I feel so connected to God and prayer at a young age? Was it my grandmother's influence, or just an ancient memory my soul carried?

When we reached our destination, Saint Anne Cathedral rose before us like a physical manifestation of prayer, its dome reaching toward heaven with the same yearning I felt in my best allegro dance jumps. This cathedral was extraordinary in its shape, beauty, light, and wisdom. I had never seen or felt anything like this, but I felt deeply connected to this moment, as if my cells recognized a frequency my mind couldn't quite name.

Inside the cathedral, the cool air carried whispers of thousands of prayers spoken over decades. Candles flickered in red glass holders, creating dancing shadows on ancient walls. But it was what I saw hanging in the middle of a rainbow-colored arc in the cathedral that stopped me mid-breath. I remember stopping mid-step, my hand reaching instinctively for my grandmother's arm. "Look up," I said with a curious smile on my face.

Hanging along the chapel walls were crutches, back braces, and other medical devices left behind by those who had found healing in this sacred space. Among them was a back brace nearly identical to the one I'd hurled across my bedroom weeks earlier.

"Babci, look," I whispered, pointing to the brace. The sound of my voice seemed to dissolve into the vastness of the space, becoming one with centuries of whispered prayers.

Her weathered hand covered mine, warm and certain. "This is why we're here, Gina," she said, her eyes holding mine with the steadiness of absolute conviction. "I knew there was something for you on this trip, for you to see, and that you're not alone in this. God hears every prayer, even the angry ones.

As I stood in that magnificent cathedral, surrounded by physical evidence of others who had walked paths similar to mine, something profound shifted within me. My prayer that day wasn't just words whispered into sacred space; it was a conversation with the divine that lived in my very cells. I moved beyond asking for my scoliosis to disappear and instead asked for the wisdom to understand why this path had been chosen for me.

"God," I prayed, my hand resting on the smooth wood of the pew before me, "help me see the purpose in this challenge. Show me how to use it rather than fight against it."

This sacred moment marked the beginning of a profound transformation in my relationship with God. The divine wasn't just an external force to petition through memorized prayers but a presence flowing through every curved and straight line of my being. It was miraculous, just like my grandmother used to say: "Miracles are everywhere." And in that moment, I knew my journey with scoliosis wasn't about conquering it at all.

It was about learning to dance with it, letting my unique geometry create its own beautiful patterns across the studio floor. My teachers began to notice something unusual in my movement quality, a distinctive way of approaching balance and alignment that came from years of adapting to my body's asymmetry. What had once been my greatest fear had become part of my artistic signature.

Just like one of my favorite childhood movies from Mary Poppins taught us, every problem has a solution, though sometimes the solution isn't what we expect but something altogether more beautiful. That twelve-year-old girl, hurling her brace against the wall in desperate prayer disguised as defiance, could never have imagined the layers of protection and grace that surrounded her.

My grandmother's wisdom showed me that God was as real as the sun and moon, her love illuminating the sacred in every step of my journey. "God doesn't make mistakes, Gina," she told me on our last day in Quebec, her voice gentle but firm. "Sometimes what looks like a burden is actually a blessing in disguise."

I saw my mother's sacrifices like driving me to and from dance classes and how they painted my world with possibilities she herself never had. Her determination was a daily reminder that love knows no bounds. Every early morning, every late night, every mile driven between Batavia and Buffalo was a testament to the kind of love, the kind of blessing, that sees future blossoms in present buds.

I received a new set of eyes on that pilgrimage, a new way to see myself and my curve. It wasn't a punishment after all, but a way for me to learn what courage and faith truly were. After five years of wearing the plastic cage sixteen hours a day, I was finally able to retire it to the corner of my closet like a costume from a role I no longer played. Dance remained my testament to this truth: Some gifts arrive wrapped in challenges, their true value revealed only through the patient unfolding of time and trust. Your perceived flaws are not divine mistakes, but sacred signatures designed to shape your unique contribution to the world.

REVIVING THE SPIRIT

Reminders

Trust the divine geometry: What appears as imperfection in your life, whether physical, emotional, or circumstantial, may actually be sacred architecture. The curves, the asymmetries, the unexpected turns are not mistakes to be fixed but unique designs with purpose.

Honor your authentic anger: Your frustration and questioning are not spiritual failures but necessary parts of genuine faith. The moment I hurled my brace across the room was not a rejection of God but an honest prayer. Allow yourself to express genuine feelings to the divine, trusting that a relationship strong enough to hear your anger is strong enough to guide your healing.

Seek evidence of companionship: The sight of other back braces hanging in that cathedral showed me I wasn't alone in my struggle. Whether through support groups, mentors, or historical examples, knowing others have navigated similar curves can transform isolation into community.

STEPS

Lipstick: Courage to express truth. Stand before your mirror and trace with loving fingers the unique contours of your body, the asymmetries and differences you've been conditioned to hide. With bold courage, declare: "These features are not flaws, they are my divine signature, my unique contribution to this world's beauty."

Lashes: Divine perspective shift. Open your eyes to see evidence of divine presence in your challenges. Where might grace be appearing unexpectedly in your current struggle? Look for the "back braces hanging in the cathedral" of your own story.

God: Connection to divine support. Remember that the divine choreographer has written your story with perfect precision, every curve a unique moment for grace. Your path isn't a mistake to be corrected but a journey to be honored. Trust that even what feels like limitation now may later reveal itself as your most powerful gift.

PRAYER

Finding Courage in Vulnerability

God of Strength and Tenderness,

In moments of vulnerability, remind me that true courage exists as faithful movement despite fear. When I feel exposed or uncertain, help me see these feelings as doorways to deeper understanding.

Grant me bravery to be seen in my truth, to stand in my unique light, to speak from my heart even when my voice trembles. Transform my vulnerable places into sources of greatest strength.

Help me recognize that what appears as imperfection may actually be sacred architecture. Show me how my unique design serves my greatest purpose.

With ease, please, turn my fears into pathways of faith, my curves into signatures of grace.

Amen.

ANGELS IN THE SKY

"When pain knocks you down, look up. Your angels carry messages that lift you higher than you could rise alone. Divine guidance rarely arrives in expected packaging." GP

Finding Grace Through Pain
Age 14 | Buffalo, New York

The inspirational lyrics of "(It's Gonna Be a) Great Day" floated through my bedroom: "When you're down and out, lift up your head and shout: There's gonna be a great day!" The 1990s cassette tape was wearing thin from constant rewinding, but those words of encouragement had become the self-talk I desperately needed wearing that rigid plastic shell that held my spine in place. The song's uplifting message about overcoming challenges and looking forward to better days ahead became my personal anthem, the musical score to my daily battle against my body's limitations.

I had heard at a young age that when the student is ready, the teacher will appear. One afternoon, at the

David DeMarie Dance studio, the late winter sunlight slanting through the windows to create golden pathways across the polished floor, I found this wisdom manifesting before my eyes. After a few years of picking the same teacher to choreograph my solo, a new dance teacher appeared at the exact moment I wanted to ask her to be my choreographer. Being the high achiever I was, spine curved but spirit determined, I knew she was the teacher I needed that year. I didn't know why I knew it was her, but you know when your inner voice is telling you something and you don't need a reason ... Well, this intuition was strong, and I was going to follow it.

The studio air always shifted when she entered, as if molecules of possibility suddenly filled the space. Her presence tall, strong, and graceful was a physical manifestation of hope. Her movements exemplified how I wanted to dance someday. During our private rehearsals, the familiar scent of her subtle perfume mingling with the rosin particles that floated in the air like fairy dust, she would demonstrate a movement with such effortless joy that my body would involuntarily respond, momentarily forgetting its constraints.

Her voice, carrying the perfect blend of technical instruction and spiritual invitation, allowed me to feel safe and at ease during each private lesson. "Feel the music in your spine, Gina," she would say. "Let it flow through every vertebra, even the ones that want to curve." And somehow, when she said it, my body believed it was possible. I knew she was the teacher I needed, and we were cosmically aligned to find each other at this precise moment in time. The universe had orchestrated this partnership with divine precision, her strength complimenting my determination, her gentleness balancing my frustration.

I don't know if you've ever experienced such perfect timing, but I knew without doubt that she was a gift from God. You see, what we listen to again and again and again becomes the thoughts we think about again and again and again. The music becomes the mind's monologue. When my solo song was chosen called, "(It's Gonna Be a) Great Day," I knew these words would get me through this final year of "The Brace." I would play that cassette until the magnetic tape threatened to snap, ensuring each battement, each arabesque, each turn conveyed the emotion this piece demanded on stage. And what I realized is the innate connection I had to this song brought something naturally out of me, so that it didn't feel like work at all. It was as if the song was my own words, lifting me up through the internal challenges I was experiencing.

At sixteen, I didn't understand this principle with the clarity I possess now. My dance teacher likely didn't realize the song she chose would become the key to unlocking the negative thoughts I harbored about my body. On the outside, I was the picture of teenage resilience, smiling through discomfort, joking about my "turtle shell," showing the world a carefully choreographed performance of positivity. But inside, I was executing a different dance altogether, battling fear that gripped my chest during quiet moments, anger that burned in my throat when I couldn't move as others did, anxiety that tingled through my limbs before doctor appointments, and a sadness that sat heavy in my solar plexus and weighed down each breath.

Dance became my healing medicine that year. The wooden studio floor became my therapist's couch; the mirrors, my confessionals; the music, my prayer. Each plié stretched not just my muscles but my capacity for patience. Each relevé lifted not just my heels but my spirits. Each pirouette taught me not just about spotting but about focusing on what mattered most. The studio became a sanctuary where my body, despite its rebellion, could speak its truth through movement. It was the exact medicine my mind and body needed to navigate the emotional turbulence this young sixteen-year-old was experiencing.

That competition season, I shined with a light that surprised even me. The stage lights caught the aurora-colored rhinestones on my costume, lovingly hand-made specifically for me, each crystal placed with intention to accentuate my movements rather than hide my brace. The blue fabric flowed like water around my body as I danced, creating the illusion of freedom even as plastic gripped my torso beneath. I felt that song in the marrow of my bones, in the curve of my spine, in the chambers of my heart as if it were essential for my survival. Because it was. It was how I survived the physical pain, the daily discomfort, the overwhelming fear, the heartbreak of not knowing if dance would remain a possibility for my body. Either way, my spirit felt revived again and again. I would practice without complaining or even feeling like it was work. That year, dance and my solo were the gift, the prescription my body followed without hesitation, and the results were extraordinary.

At the end of that year, when the doctor finally said, "Gina, you're done with the brace," I expected elation to wash over me like a cleansing rain. Instead, I felt strangely numb, my emotions suspended in a state of disbelief. The brace that had been both my prison and my protection. With it suddenly gone, I was left vulnerable in ways I hadn't anticipated.

I thought that when the doctor told me my spine had healed and I was free from the plastic cage, happiness would flood through me, washing away all the negative emotions like a spiritual baptism. On the outside, they did disappear, as I smiled with fake excitement. But on inside, I felt hollow, confused by my own response to this long-awaited freedom.

I was utterly unprepared for this emotional paradox. Have you ever experienced that disconnect? When external circumstances say you should be celebrating, but your internal landscape remains covered in fog? When the test results come back clear or the doctor gives you the all-clear, but the emotional residue of fear remains, like a ghost haunting your body's memory?

I suppose I was meant to give those lingering feelings to God. But what does that actually mean, to give your worries or fears to God? What tangible action translates the spiritual instruction into emotional relief? Faced with uncertainty, I did what I knew how to do: I prayed with the passion of a good Catholic girl, hands clasped so tightly my knuckles whitened, and then continued with the coping mechanism I had mastered. I pushed down all those complicated feelings that threatened to drag me under, applied another coat of emotional waterproofing, and kept moving forward. I applied my lipstick and lashes both literally and metaphorically, learning the time-honored feminine tradition of suppression and carry on. The 1990s weren't exactly the golden age of emotional intelligence or mental health awareness. It wasn't anyone's fault. We simply didn't have the language or tools to process what couldn't be seen on an x-ray.

I carried on just like everyone else. I did what any overachiever with a newly straight-enough spine would do. I doubled down on school and dance, channeling all my energy into measurable achievements where success could be quantified by grades and trophies. I continued to show the world how strong Gina Pero was. Only my bedroom walls witnessed how angry, confused, and afraid I sometimes felt. If they could talk, they'd have quite the story to tell. The following year brought a new physical outlet, when my father encouraged me to play basketball while continuing to dance. If you're a basketball fan, you know the exhilaration the game can bring. I absolutely fell in love with the game, the squeak of sneakers against the polished court, the satisfying swish of a perfect shot, the strategic chess match of offense and defense, the competitive energy that made my heart race in the best possible way.

I became a fiery defensive player, my body once constrained by a brace now diving across hardwood floors to prevent the opposing team from advancing. This experience gifted me with presence, with the joy of being part of something larger than myself, with teammates working in synchronized motion toward a common goal. Basketball provided the perfect outlet for all that bedroom anger. The physical exertion and controlled aggression of the sport allowed emotions to flow through movement rather than remain trapped in my body.

You're welcome, bedroom walls. And thank you, God, for a father who loved basketball and became one of the best coaches in Batavia, New York. His passion for the game opened a new avenue of healing for me, though neither of us recognized it as such at the time. Go, Dad! One particular game stands out in my memory. I can still hear the squeal of rubber soles against polished wood, the soundtrack to a pivotal moment. We were down by two points. Halftime was approaching, just one minute away on the countdown clock. I glanced toward the bleachers where my mother sat, her eyes following every movement on the court with the intensity that only a mother can summon.

"Mom," I called out during a brief pause in play, "at halftime we're leaving. Remember I have to go dance. I already told my coach I need to go."

My mother's eyes narrowed slightly, a look I knew all too well, the one that meant negotiations were not an option. "Gina," she replied, her voice carrying across the gymnasium with surprising clarity, "there's no way we're leaving. You're down by two, and the team needs you."

Walking to the locker room, frustration building with each step, I knew I had no choice in the matter. My mother's competitive spirit, the same one she had passed down to me, had made the decision. It was what it was. When the third quarter whistle blew, I stormed onto the court with renewed determination, ready to close that two-point gap and get to my dance class.

The ball found its way to me. I saw an opening and took it, my body responding with the quick reflexes dance had helped me develop. I was running for what should have been a perfect layup when suddenly the opposing team's taller, more substantial forward appeared like a wall before me. The collision was inevitable, violent in its unexpectedness. I went down to the ground, my left ankle rolling beneath me, creating a sickening sensation I can still feel when I recall the moment.

White-hot pain shot up my leg as I clutched my ankle, tears streaming down my face. My coach rushed over to help me off the floor, and I found myself benched with ice pressed against my rapidly swelling joint. Through the haze of pain, disbelief coursed through me alongside the throbbing working its way up my leg.

I was supposed to leave at halftime. I was supposed to be in the car by now, my mother driving me to the dance studio where my body knew how to move without betraying me. I shot a look at my mom, part accusation, part plea for help as my dad helped me to the car, an ice pack still clutched to my ankle.

We drove straight to dance class anyway, hope and denial battling within me. Perhaps it wasn't as bad as it felt. Perhaps I could dance through it, as I had danced through so many other challenges. But the moment I tried to put weight on my hurt foot, reality crashed down upon me. Trying to push through class, I finally surrendered to the inevitable, sinking to the floor as tears of defeat tracked silently down my cheeks. If the swelling didn't subside by morning, I knew what awaited me: another doctor, another diagnosis, another detour in my physical journey.

Morning brought no miracle. Off to the doctor we went, the waiting room's antiseptic smell now as familiar to me as the scent of my own home. The x-ray confirmed my worst fears: a chip fracture. The doctor's words blurred together until the phrase "date for surgery" snapped me back to attention. The medicine called dance, my most reliable prescription for emotional wellbeing, was suddenly contraindicated. I was stripped of the very thing that had made getting out of bed possible during my darkest days with the back brace.

The pain that followed existed on multiple levels, each layer more complex than the last. The physical pain of my fractured ankle shot through me like lightning splits the sky, bright and jagged and impossible to ignore. But it was the emotional pain that threatened to undo me completely. The pain of not being able to walk independently, of being thrust back into dependency after finally tasting freedom from my back brace.

The complicated pain I felt toward my mother, anger mingled with guilt for even allowing myself to feel that anger. The guilt doubled because I knew she couldn't have predicted the injury, that she only wanted what was best for me and the team.

And the pain of not knowing how to manage the emotions that overflowed within me while I simultaneously tried to present a brave face to my family.

The cosmic irony of wearing an ankle brace so soon after shedding my back brace left me questioning God's plan with renewed intensity. The fear of surgery, of surrendering control of my body to someone who would literally screw my ankle back together, kept me awake at night, staring at shadow patterns on my bedroom ceiling.

The pain continued to evolve as I healed, weighed down by the anxiety of standing on two feet again, afraid to trust my own body. There was also the logistical nightmare of navigating high school on crutches, backpack awkwardly slung over one shoulder, books clutched precariously against my chest, the constant calculation of how to get from A to B before the bell rang. And the reluctant surrender of independence, as I had to accept help from classmates and teachers, when everything in me had been trained to prove I could do it all myself.

The pain of uncertainty about my future stretched before me like an uncharted road. The physical discomfort that radiated from my ankle up my legs and into my lower back, as my body tried to compensate for its newest challenge. Finding a comfortable position became a never-ending quest, comfort as elusive as certainty.

The pain, the pain, the pain that no one else could see. On the outside, I maintained the appearance of resilience, my lipstick perfectly applied, my lashes framing determined eyes, my smile suggesting all was well. But inside, I was drowning in a sea of pain that threatened to pull me under.

So, I returned to the song that had carried me through my back brace journey. As I lay with my elevated ankle, I pressed play on that worn cassette once more. When Barbra sang "When you're down and out, lift up your head and shout," I realized the song wasn't promising that hard times wouldn't come but offering a way through them. The line "angels in the sky promise that by and by" wasn't about magical intervention but about finding faith in future possibilities even when present circumstances seemed bleak. The lyrics washed over me like a baptism, and the message about staying hopeful during difficult times, about the promise of better days ahead, became my lifeline once more.

The lyrics reminded me that even in our darkest moments, we are not alone. That divine messengers surround us, whether they appear as dance teachers, fathers who introduce us to new passions, or simply as a perfect song arriving at the perfect moment. They promised that no matter how painful the present moment, it would not last forever. That beyond today's struggles lie tomorrow's joys.

Each time I played that cassette, wearing down the magnetic tape with repetition, I was actually rewiring my brain, creating new neural pathways of trust and faith. The music became more than sound: It became prayer, therapy, and meditation rolled into one. Each time I sang along, even through tears, I was declaring my refusal to be defined by limitation.

Lying in my bedroom with my elevated ankle, I realized that perhaps these physical challenges weren't punishments but opportunities, doorways to depths of resilience I might never have discovered otherwise. My scoliosis and my fractured ankle weren't just medical conditions to overcome but teachers guiding me toward a more profound understanding of my own strength.

As I hummed along with Barbra's powerful crescendo, something shifted inside me. I finally understood what the song had been teaching me all along. Lyrics like "There's gonna be a great day" weren't a guarantee of perfect days; they were a reminder that even in our darkest moments, we can choose to look up and find light. The pain didn't disappear, but it became bearable, contextualized within a larger story of becoming. I wasn't just a girl with a curved spine and a broken ankle. I was a dancer, a basketball player, a daughter, a student, a friend, and above all a spirit, learning to navigate the physical world with grace, even when that grace came with crutches.

REVIVING THE SPIRIT

Reminders

Hear the music behind the noise: When life's challenges create dissonance and pain, listen more deeply for the harmony of possibility that plays beneath it all. Just as the lyrics became my lifeline, there is always a message of truth waiting to sustain you through difficult passages. Train your spiritual ears to hear the encouragement.

Welcome the divine messengers: Teachers appear in many forms, some as teachers, others as songs that speak directly to your soul. Stay open to guidance that arrives in unexpected packages, recognizing that divine help often wears everyday disguises. The angels mentioned in the song were simply ordinary people carrying extraordinary messages.

Embrace the rhythm of release: Sometimes the most powerful healing comes from honest emotional expression your expressed pain is the necessary prelude to resilience, creating space for new neural pathways of faith and trust to form.

STEPS

🥢 Lipstick: Express courageous truth. When pain knocks you down, reapply your courage by selecting a song that speaks to your spirit and play it daily until its message becomes part of your internal dialogue.

👁 Lashes: See divine messengers. Look for the teachers, and basketball-loving fathers, those angels disguised in everyday form appearing precisely when needed. See through the lens of divine choreography and open your eyes to recognize how it's arranging people and circumstances for your growth.

✦ God: Connect with God's perfect schedule. Divine timing doesn't always match our preferred schedule. The next time you find yourself asking "Why now?" or "Why me?" take a deep breath and add: "Show me what I need to learn from this." Trust that your pain is not random but purposeful, even when the purpose remains temporarily hidden. Consider that God might be more interested in your spiritual growth than your immediate comfort. The universe conspires in mysterious ways to help us grow, and sometimes growth comes wrapped in challenges that only reveal their gifts with time and trust.

PRAYER

A Prayer for Perspective

Divine Choreographer of Life,

Teach me to see each misstep as guidance, each stumble as a teacher, each fall as preparation for rising stronger. When my perspective narrows, expand my vision to encompass Your greater design.

Help me transform moments of imbalance into movements of insight, experiences of uncertainty into expansions of wisdom. Grant me the ability to see beauty in unexpected places and recognize angels in human form.

When challenges cloud my vision, clear my sight to perceive divine messages within. Let me view my journey through grace rather than judgment.

With ease, please, help me trust life's choreography and find meaning in every step. Amen.

THE SENSITIVE SOUL

"Your sensitivity isn't a weakness to overcome but a gift to embrace. It is the very quality that allows you to connect deeply with art, nature, and the authentic needs of others." GP

Finding My Voice Through Movement
Age 5 | Batavia, New York

In my earliest memories, my father was a mountain solid, unwavering, and impossibly tall. His arms were my first sanctuary, a place where the world's sharp edges softened into whispers. The comforting scent of his aftershave mingled with the laundry detergent my mother used on his shirts created a fragrant embrace that signaled safety before I even had words for what safety meant. I would burrow into his embrace, again and again, clinging with an intensity that puzzled even me, my small fingers gripping his shirt as if it were the only stable thing in a spinning world.

Something deep within my young soul recognized him as my anchor in a world that felt overwhelming in ways I couldn't yet articulate. Colors seemed too vibrant, sounds too jarring, emotions both mine and others' like relentless waves that sometimes threatened to pull me under. While my parents saw a shy child who needed protection, the truth was far more complex. I was a sensitive spirit learning to navigate a world that felt too bright, too loud, too much. My nervous system seemed to lack the natural filters others possessed, leaving me raw and receptive to every nuance of energy around me.

"She is just shy," my mother would say, her voice gentle but concerned as her eyes followed my movements while I carefully avoided the chaotic energy of a family gathering. Only years later would I recognize the profound truth no one around me seemed to understand that my apparent withdrawal from the world resulted from a sense of being profoundly overwhelmed by it."

Kindergarten loomed before me like an insurmountable wall, its approach making my heart flutter like a trapped bird beneath my ribs. That first morning, I stood frozen at the classroom doorway, my small hands locked around my parents' fingers as if they were lifelines to safety. The fluorescent lights buzzed overhead with an intensity others seemed oblivious to, their harsh glow making the edges of everything too sharp, too defined. The noise of children's voices bounced off walls painted with primary colors that seemed to vibrate with uncomfortable intensity, and every cell in my body screamed to retreat.

My kindergarten teacher, with wisdom that would have made the famous nanny from the film Mary Poppins proud, knelt to meet my eyes. The gentle lines around her mouth softened as she smiled, extending a Chips Ahoy chocolate chip cookie that still warms my heart when I think of it (although today a fresh batch of whole ingredient cookies are the ones I prefer). That chocolate chip cookie became a sweet bridge between fear and possibility. That spoonful of sugar indeed helped the medicine go down as Mary Poppins would say coaxing me into a world, I wasn't sure I was ready to enter.

Inside the classroom, I became a quiet observer, perched on my tiny chair like a small bird ready to take flight at the first sudden sound. My fingers would trace the smooth wood grain of the desk, finding comfort in its predictable patterns, while the unpredictable energy of twenty-five children swirled around me like a hurricane. My eyes constantly drifted to the windows, seeking comfort in the gentle sway of maple tree branches and the promise of recess, when I could finally breathe freely under the open sky. The outside world called to me with a voice I understood better than the chatter around me, a silent language of wind and sunlight that felt more like home than any human conversation.

"Gina is just shy," my teachers would tell my parents during conferences, as if discussing a condition that required treatment. "She will grow through this." What they couldn't understand was that my apparent withdrawal wasn't absence but the presence of a heightened awareness that made ordinary social interaction overwhelming. I wasn't missing the world; I was experiencing too much of it, each emotion, each energy, each subtle shift in the room's dynamic registering in my body like changes in atmospheric pressure before a storm. Why wasn't anyone able to identify what was really going on?

Nap time brought its own kind of solace, especially with my Mark nearby, a familiar family friend I had known since birth. We'd lay our thin blue mats close together on the cool linoleum floor, finding comfort in the simple presence of another soul who seemed to understand the language of silence. In those quiet moments, when the fluorescent lights were mercifully dimmed, questions far too profound for my young age would float through my mind: Why did everything feel so intense? Why did others move through the world with such ease, while I felt every interaction like a stone dropped in still water? Why did I feel so different, so apart from the whirlwind of activity around me?

These weren't just a child's wanderings, they were the stirrings of an old soul trying to remember its purpose in this new, small body. It was as if I had arrived in the world with knowledge I couldn't quite access, wisdom that hummed beneath the surface of my consciousness like a familiar melody played just beyond hearing range.

Then came the day that changed everything: my first dance class at Miss Suzanne's School of Dance. My mother, forever searching for activities that might "bring me out of my shell," had enrolled me with more hope than expectation. The studio door opened to reveal a space unlike any I'd encountered before. Warm wooden floors stretched beneath my feet, absorbing sound rather than amplifying it. Natural light poured through tall windows, creating pools of gold across the room rather than the harsh glare of institutional fluorescents. The studio floor beneath my feet felt like holy ground, and the mirror reflected back something I had never seen before: a child completely at home in her own skin.

The first tentative positions, feet turned out in first position, arms forming a gentle oval before me, felt like coming home to a place I'd always known but never visited. My body understood this language instinctively, as if remembering rather than learning. When I stepped onto a stage for the first time nine months later, something ancient and powerful awakened within me. The spotlight created a sacred circle that held just me and the music, the audience fading into a comfortable darkness beyond its edges. This wasn't just movement; it was communion with something larger than myself. In dance, I found a language that could express everything my young heart held but couldn't speak.

What everyone had labeled as shyness was actually a deep sensitivity to the unseen currents of life, the emotional undertones in conversations, the subtle dynamics between people, the shifting energies in a room. On stage, this sensitivity transformed from a burden into a gift. Each movement became a prayer, each gesture a conversation with something greater than myself. The music moved through me like breath, articulating truths I had no words for. I wasn't emerging from a shell; I was finally finding a way to translate my soul's language into something the world could understand.

"It's like watching a different child," my mother whispered to my father during my first recital, tears catching the stage lights as they slid down her cheeks. They had expected dance to "fix" my shyness, to make me more like other children. What they witnessed instead was revelation, the emergence not of a new personality but of an authentic self that had always been there, waiting for the right language to express its truth.

Dance became my medicine, but not in the way people might think. It wasn't about curing shyness or fixing what others perceived as a problem. Instead, it was about discovering the truth of who I was meant to be. When I danced, energy coursed through me like lightning through summer clouds, each movement a perfect marriage of discipline and freedom. My spirit, which had always felt too big for ordinary interactions, finally had room to expand, to soar, to speak its truth through movement.

In plié, I found humility, the power of bending without breaking. In relevé, I discovered the joy of reaching upward while remaining grounded. In pirouette, I learned to focus on finding stillness within motion by keeping my eyes fixed on a single point through the turn. These weren't just dance techniques; they were life philosophies encoded in physical form, pieces of wisdom my body understood before my mind could comprehend them.

What looked like transformation to the outside world was actually recognition of self. I wasn't becoming something new; I was remembering something ancient. That little girl who couldn't enter a kindergarten classroom without a cookie wasn't shy at all. She was an empath, a sensitive soul, already tuned to frequencies others couldn't hear. Dance didn't change who I was; it revealed me.

The music flowed through me like a current of pure energy, each note resonating in a different part of my body: bass notes grounding through my feet, melodies swirling through my arms, harmonies expanding my chest until my heart felt too big for my ribcage. For the first time, I felt truly seen for who I was, no longer the shy girl who clung to her father but the deep feeling soul who could absorb the world's emotions and transform them into art.

In dance, I discovered that what others had labeled as a problem was actually my gift. The sensitivity that made ordinary interaction overwhelming allowed me to feel music in ways others couldn't, not just hearing the notes but experiencing them as colors, as textures, as emotions that moved through my body like water seeking its natural path. While the world saw a shy child who struggled to connect, I was actually a deeply feeling soul who experienced connection so intensely that it could be overwhelming without the right channel for expression.

With every leap, every turn, every graceful movement, I felt my spirit soar free from the constraints that bound it in ordinary interaction. The arabesque standing on one leg while extending the other behind me, arms reaching forward into infinite possibility became a physical manifestation of emotional release. Dance became more than just an activity; it was my medicine, my meditation, my way of channeling the profound sensitivity that had once seemed like a burden.

On stage, that sensitivity transformed into something beautiful, like a prism that doesn't diminish light but instead reveals its hidden colors. The energy that had once overwhelmed me now flowed through me with purpose, telling stories through movement that words could never fully express. My body, which had once felt like a too-fragile vessel for such intense feelings, became a strong and capable instrument, translating emotion into art with every precisely executed movement.

The truth was beginning to emerge, unfolding like a tightly closed flower finally receiving the right combination of light and nourishment: I wasn't shy at all. I was an empath, a soul who felt the world's emotions as if they were my own, who could sense the invisible currents that ran beneath the surface of ordinary interaction. My sensitivity wasn't a weakness to overcome but a strength to embrace, a gift to be channeled rather than suppressed.

That little girl clutching her father's arm wasn't afraid of the world; she was learning to navigate her gift of deep emotional perception. The warmth of his embrace wasn't just comfort, it was teaching her about the healing power of safe connection, a lesson she would later translate into movement that could touch hearts and heal spirits. Through dance, I discovered that being highly empathic wasn't a flaw to fix but a superpower to channel. The stage became my sanctuary, the place where my sensitivity could shine, where the depth of my feeling nature could be expressed in its purest form. Now I understand that those early experiences weren't about shyness at all. They were the first steps of an empath learning to dance with her gift, finding her way to transform overwhelming sensitivity into graceful strength. The journey from my father's protective embrace to center stage wasn't about becoming something different, it was about discovering what had been there all along, waiting for the right conditions to blossom.

In the end, dance didn't change who I was; it revealed who I'd been all along: not a shy child, but a deeply feeling soul who needed the right language to speak her truth. The stage didn't cure my sensitivity; it transformed what the world had labeled as a problem into what God had always intended as a gift.

REVIVING THE SPIRIT

Reminders

Honor your sensitivity as divine design: What others may label as shyness, oversensitivity, or introversion may actually be a spiritual gift of deep perception. Your ability to feel deeply to sense energies, emotions, and subtleties is a sacred capacity to nurture.

Find your sacred language: Just as dance became my way to translate internal experience into external expression, there is a medium, practice, or form of expression uniquely suited to your spirit. Your divine language is the one that makes you feel most fully alive and authentically present.

Trust your body's wisdom: Your physical form holds intelligence that often precedes conscious understanding. Your physical responses, tension, ease, contraction, and expansion are not random but meaningful communications from your deepest self.

STEPS

Lipstick: Express your sensitive truth. "My sensitivity is my superpower." Your ability to feel deeply is divine design, not disorder. Today, wear your sensitivity as confidently as your favorite shade of lipstick, or lip balm. It's a defining feature of your authentic beauty.

Lashes: See through empathic eyes. Look with new eyes at the aspects of yourself that you've been told to change or hide. Look at yourself through a lens of divine design rather than societal expectation. Your unique perspective is a gift to the world, not a problem to overcome.

God: Connect through your sensitivity. The divine choreographer crafted your heightened awareness with perfect intention. Your sensitive spirit, your ability to absorb and process emotion, your need for a safe space to express your truth these are all intentional aspects of your sacred design. Today, place your hand on your heart and whisper: "Thank you for making me a feeling soul in a world that needs more deep feeling." Trust that your unique sensitivities are preparing you for your unique purpose.

PRAYER

A Prayer for the Sensitive Soul

Divine Creator of Delicate Perception,

Thank You for crafting me with senses that feel the world deeply. You have blessed me with sacred awareness and profound strength disguised as sensitivity.

Guide me toward the sacred language of my soul movement, art, music, or words that transform intensity into power. Grant me courage to honor my sensitivity.

Show me my sanctuary where my spirit finds freedom, where light bathes me in warmth, where life becomes beautiful choreography. Help me recognize fellow empaths as kindred spirits with magnificent gifts. A light already shining, A gift already complete.

With ease, please, help me embrace sensitivity as my divine purpose and greatest strength.

Amen.

DIALING INTO TRUTH

"Four simple words spoken with belief can redirect a life's trajectory. Never underestimate how your expression of faith in someone else might become the light that guides them through their darkest doubts."
GP

Four Words That Changed Everything
Age 16 | Rochester, New York

Have you ever stood at a crossroads, certain you were taking your final steps away from a dream you once loved? Have you felt the weight of surrender, heavy and final, only to have your entire path redirected by four simple words spoken at precisely the right moment? This is what happened to me the day an angel disguised as a dance teacher spoke the exact words my wounded spirit needed to hear.

The question echoed through my mind constantly during that pivotal time: *What am I doing here?* It was a question that began as doubt but would transform into purpose, a refrain from the Olympic soundtrack that would become the musical backdrop to my resurrection as a dancer. But I'm getting ahead of my story.

It was the summer after my ankle surgery, my leg confined in a blue ankle brace that tied up my shins like an unwelcome corsage, nestled by two titanium screws that felt cold and foreign beneath my skin. The physical healing had progressed, bone fusing to metal, tissue knitting itself back together. But beneath the surface, a deeper questioning had taken root. Questions like, do I still dance? Do I still love dance? Do I want to continue to dance? They surfaced in my mind again and again, like waves that refused to retreat back to sea, each one eroding a bit more of my confidence. The once-clear path of my dancing future had become obscured by pain, uncertainty, and the dim afterglow of surgical lights and months spent on crutches, the rubber tips squeaking against our kitchen floor with every hobbled step.

In those strenuous days of questioning, one of my mother's friends appeared on our front porch for coffee. The steam rose from their Dunkin Donuts mugs, mingling with the morning air, as they sat in wicker chairs exchanging news. She shared that there was an intensive summer dance program happening at Little Red Dancing School in Rochester, New York, under the direction of a teacher by the name of Miss Lisa. Now, I had seen Miss Lisa's dancers at dance competitions before their technique flawless, their performance quality magnetic, their costumes catching the stage lights in ways that made them appear to glow from within. They were outstanding in every way, setting a standard that seemed impossibly high, especially now.

My body still felt foreign, as if I'd been transformed into a non-moving object, a statue of a dancer rather than the real thing. My confidence in dance was completely shattered, like a mirror dropped from a great height, impossible to reassemble into its original form. Yet my mother, with that beautiful blend of gentle persistence and unwavering belief that defined her approach to my dreams, helped me sign up for the summer dance experience.

I arrived that first day with the blue brace on my ankle announcing my limitation to everyone before I even spoke a word. Nervousness radiated through my body like electricity seeking ground. Insecurity clung to me like a second skin, damp and uncomfortable in the summer heat. The teachers were outstanding professionals from New York City with training and perspectives I had never encountered in my small-town studios. Their movements spoke a dialect of dance I recognized but couldn't speak fluently.

Dancing wasn't easy that summer. Each plié was a negotiation with gravity, my knees and ankles engaged in a heated debate about how far was safe to bend. Each relevé was a question my body wasn't sure how to answer, the rise onto the balls of my feet feeling precarious and unfamiliar. I was rediscovering how to balance, walk, turn, and jump again, the most basic dance vocabulary requiring translation in my post-surgery body.

But there was something new inside of me that was beginning to crack open, a seedling of possibility pushing through concrete doubt. The dancers around me were extraordinarily talented and getting noticed by the NYC master teachers, their praises echoing through the studio. Meanwhile, I faded to the background. Although I wanted to be noticed, I knew that if dance was something I wanted to keep doing, I had to find a different purpose than being seen. I had to rediscover what made dance essential to my spirit, not just my ego.

I thought long and hard that summer about signing up for another dance season in the fall, this time in Rochester instead of Buffalo. For the first time, living in Batavia, smack dab between the two cities, made sense to me. God's plan was perfect, and I was starting to accept it, recognizing a pattern in seemingly random events. As my mom asked me if I wanted to dance with

Miss Lisa this season, I answered, "I don't know," the words carrying the weight of dreams I wasn't sure belonged to me anymore. So I decided to attend a Wednesday night jazz session, a tentative commitment to not completely abandon the art but to slowly welcome it back in.

Each Wednesday, I would drive to Little Red Dancing School, the forty-minute journey giving me time to build my courage before arriving. There was something magical about those evenings in the small framing studio, with its wooden floors worn smooth by countless dancing feet and the enticing smell of pizza next door.

One particular Wednesday night changed everything. We were doing a balancing exercise in center floor, that vulnerable space where there are no barres to hold on to, no walls to steady yourself against, relying only on your body's wisdom to keep you upright. The studio lights seemed particularly bright that evening, highlighting every struggle, every compensation in high definition. All the dancers around me were able to balance with an effortlessness that made me feel left out. On two feet, one foot in relevé, on one leg, on two, their bodies finding that perfect alignment where gravity seemed negotiable rather than absolute.

I was struggling, my body betraying me with every wobble, every compensation, every fall out of position. Sweat beaded along my hairline not from exertion but from frustration. The mirror reflected back a dancer who couldn't find her center, whose foundation had been shattered into pieces, completely shifted like tectonic plates after an earthquake. I felt heartbroken, and not just because I couldn't balance but because everyone else in the room could. Their steady forms in the mirror served as constant reminders of what I used to be what I feared I might never be again.

Miss Lisa would come behind me and physically hold me up, her hands steady on my waist, knowing that her assistance would help me feel more secure, more confident, more aware. Her touch was gentle but firm, a reminder of what stability felt like. But when she stepped away, I would falter again, my ankle's weakness exposing my body's new limitations. The sound of my foot returning heavily to the floor after each failed attempt seemed to echo in the studio, though perhaps that was just my heightened awareness of each failure.

I left class that night, discouraged and defeated, and cried my eyes out on the drive home. No cell phones existed at the time, so there was no one to talk to but my passenger, God. The dark highway became my confessional, the car interior witnessing my surrender as tears blurred the headlights of oncoming traffic. I made a decision in the car that night: I was going to quit. I was confident in my decision. I knew dance wasn't for me anymore. The period at the end of that sentence felt final, like the game show moment: "Is that your final answer?" And I thought it was.

I got home that night, late as usual, the house quiet except for the hum of the refrigerator and the distant sound of my parents' television. I went to bed, the sheets cool against my overheated skin, sleep claiming me quickly as emotional exhaustion overrode physical fatigue. I woke up early the next morning for school, moving through the familiar routines of getting dressed and gathering books, the normality providing comfort my dancing no longer could. It was the first time I was more excited to go to school than dance.

After the final bell rang, the hallways clearing of students rushing to sports and clubs and part-time jobs, I approached my parents with my declaration. "Mom and Dad, I have decided to quit dance." The words felt heavy in my mouth, like stones I was finally settling down after carrying them too long. Their response wasn't what I expected. No arguments. No persuasion. Just a simple directive: "Well, if you want to quit dance, then you can pick up the phone," the phone connected to the wall, by the way "and call Miss Lisa yourself and tell her you quit."

So I did what any young girl would do when faced with the adult responsibility of ending her own dream at age fifteen: I picked up the phone, dialed Miss Lisa, and waited through the rings that seemed to stretch into eternity. My heart pounded in my chest, each beat seeming to say "quit-quit-quit" as I rehearsed what I would say. When Miss Lisa answered, her voice warm and familiar through the line, I blurted out my decision without hesitation, "Hi, Miss Lisa. I want to quit dancing."

The pause that followed contained universes. I could hear my own pulse in my ears, feel the coiled phone cord wrapped anxiously around my finger, cutting off circulation. Then came her response, four words that would alter the trajectory of my life. She said, "I believe in you."

I stood there, phone pressed to my ear, the coiled cord wrapped around my finger, suddenly speechless. Four words. Just four simple words had somehow reached past all my carefully constructed reasons and touched something essential within me. After another moment of silence, filled only with the sound of my own breathing, I heard myself say, "I'll see you tomorrow." I gently returned the receiver to its cradle, looked at my parents, still sitting on the living room couch, and asked, "Can I borrow the car tomorrow to go to dance?" Four words coming from a teacher's mouth changed a decision I thought I was sure of. What was it about Miss Lisa's voice that day? What was it about her response? What was it about the message I received that turned my heart around? How could four words transmute my fifteen-year-old's certainty into golden possibility? But they did, changing my resignation into determination swiftly and quickly.

When I showed up the next day, I stood and acted differently. My spine straightened with new purpose, my chin lifted slightly higher. My confidence felt new, like a garment I was trying on that somehow fit perfectly despite my doubts. The classroom that had been a place of frustration was now a sudden sanctuary I never wanted to leave, the wood floors and mirrored walls feeling like home rather than an interrogation room. And I knew Miss Lisa's "Home of Champions" her tagline was exactly where I belonged.

The car rides that had been tear-filled journeys of defeat became exciting and purposeful, with the windows down to let the wind rush through my hair and music turned up to match my rising spirits. The drives inspired me, the familiar landscape now reflecting dreams rather than limitations. The Rocky Balboa song on my cassette tape, "Eye of the Tiger," became my mental soundtrack, its driving rhythm pushing me forward.

And you know what? Even in the midst of that challenge with balance, I kept going. The wobbles continued, but now they were steps on a path rather than evidence of failure. My loss of balance became information rather than accusation and judgment. Each time my ankle gave way, I gathered data rather than shame.

That year, Miss Lisa picked out the most perfect solo song for me, called "What Am I Doing Here" from an Olympic Games soundtrack. The opening lines wondered about purpose and dreams, echoing my own search for meaning in my continued dance journey. As the song progressed, it spoke of fear falling away, of finding clarity, of being precisely where one was meant to be.

These musical questions mirrored my inner dialogue exactly: Was I meant to keep dancing? Might I stumble and fall? Could this still be my time to shine? The song captured both my vulnerability and my emerging determination. Each time I practiced to this music, its message sank deeper into my consciousness.

What struck me most powerfully were the lyrics asking the heart not to listen to the mind. This resonated so deeply: My logical mind had decided dance was over for me, but my heart never accepted that conclusion. The song acknowledged playing scenarios out "a thousand times," exactly what I had been doing during those tear-filled car rides, imagining life without dance, trying to convince myself it was for the best.

When I danced to the part about becoming fully aware and memorizing everything, I found myself doing exactly that. Noticing every sensation, every muscle engagement, every moment of connection with the music in a way I never had before my injury. The surgery had forced me to dance with new awareness, and the song celebrated this as a gift rather than a limitation.

Through Miss Lisa's belief in me, she had taught me that giving my best was the only thing that truly mattered. Not being the best compared to others, but offering the best that I uniquely had to give. The song's message about having "no place I'd rather be" became increasingly true with each passing day in the studio.
These words were my story, the articulation of the struggle I was going through that year. But in the choreography that Miss Lisa designed just for me, they became more than questions, they became mindful

affirmations of possibility. The music that had initially voiced my doubts now carried me through them, each note lifting me higher than my fears could reach. The message that had named my fears now helped me face them and keep going, providing a soundtrack to my resurrection as a dancer.

Miss Lisa's four words, "I believe in you," made me feel like I was being guided by a holy spirit, made me open to hearing what I needed to hear to keep going, keep striving, and keep following my passion even as my mind was telling me it would have been so much easier to let it go. Her voice had become the counterpoint to my doubts, a harmony strong enough to transform the entire melody of my self-perception.

For the first time, I understood that it wasn't about my plan, but about God's plan. Miss Lisa was the angel who was helping me see one dance step at a time, illuminating just enough of the path ahead for me to take the next step with courage. Like a flashlight in darkness, she didn't reveal the entire journey at once, which would have been overwhelming, but just enough ground for me to move forward.

The summer that followed brought unexpected triumphs. At national competitions, I found myself standing among the top ten contestants. Miss Lisa's four words had transformed not just my dancing but my entire understanding of faith, perseverance, and divine guidance.

Miss Lisa's four words became the foundation upon which I rebuilt the relationship with my body, my own spirit, and the divine plan that was unfolding through every stumble and triumph. In learning to give my best, whether centered or falling, succeeding or failing, it persuaded my mind to join my heart in continuing to choose dance. The inner argument between head and heart was finally resolved, not through elimination of one voice but through the creation of harmony between the two, a duet rather than competing solos.

Sometimes quitting feels like the only logical choice, but logic alone without the heart cannot navigate the sacred territory of your deepest calling.

REVIVING THE SPIRIT

Reminders

The power of verbal expression: Four simple words, "I believe in you," spoken with authentic conviction, can redirect a life's trajectory. Never underestimate how your expression of faith in someone else might become the light that guides them through their darkest doubts.

Trust the divine timing of teachers: When you find yourself questioning everything you once knew for certain, pay attention to who appears in your life. The universe sends exactly the right guides at exactly the right moments. These divine appointments arrive right on time.

Allow your questions to become your pathway: The very doubts that seem to signal the end of a dream can become the necessary clearing that allows a deeper, more authentic relationship with that dream to emerge. Empowered questions, just like the question in the song, "What am I doing here?" can open up the heart to know your authentic answer.

STEPS

Lipstick: Using four empowering words of your choice like, "I believe in me" or "I know I can," can help your self talk become the sacred power to reframe your verbal language..

Lashes: Look for the Miss Lisas in your life, those people who see potential in you that you may have stopped seeing in yourself. Who has spoken words of belief over you? Who has held you up when you couldn't balance on your own? Who might need you to be their Miss Lisa today? Whose wobbly balance might need your steady hands and affirming words?

God: The divine plan rarely unfolds according to our timeline or expectations. Today, identify one area where you've been trying to force your own plan rather than allowing God's choreography to guide you. Then listen for the quiet response; it may come as a song lyric, a memory, or simply a sense of peace about taking just the next single step.

PRAYER

The Power of Divine Affirmation

Creator of Divine Messages,

Thank You for speaking through human voices when doubts overwhelm me. Thank You for placing angels in my path, disguised as teachers and friends who see what I cannot yet see in myself.

Help me remember that challenges, physical, emotional, or circumstantial, are not random burdens but sacred containers shaping my unique gifts. Grant me the vision to see how difficulties prepare my most authentic offering.

When logic battles with heart wisdom, help me surrender to beautiful redirections. Give me courage to stand taller each day, ears to hear Your loving words through countless voices.

With ease, please, grant me grace to speak affirming words to others, becoming the angel someone needs. Amen.

Part Two: The Performance

Where external success meets internal questioning and divine redirection

"The stages grow larger, the spotlights brighter, yet the questions deeper until what appears to be knocking you down is actually aligning you with your true calling. Sometimes the most profound redirection comes when your rehearsed dance is divinely interrupted."

The Next Step

"When you cannot see the entire staircase, having faith in the next step is enough. Trust that a single step taken with commitment will open into possibilities you couldn't have imagined from where you stand now."
GP

Finding Faith in the Present
Age 18-22 | Batavia and Buffalo, New York

The heavy scent of the 1990s famous hairspray, Aquanet, hung in the high school hallways like invisible fog, mingling with the particular blend of teenage perfume, gym shorts, and cafeteria food that still defines those formative years for me. Fluorescent lights buzzed overhead, casting a sterile glow that seemed to expose not just my face but all my uncertainties. Leaning against my locker, the cool metal pressing through my shirt, I watched as classmates with confident strides and clear destinations moved past me, while I remained frozen in indecision.

Questions about my future circled my mind like storm clouds dark and threatening to unleash a downpour of anxiety at any moment. What are you going to do with your future? Are you going to college? What will you major in? What are you going to study? What will you become? The thunder and lightning of expectations came from all angles my family, teachers, counselors, friends creating a storm system of pressure that felt impossible to navigate.

My stomach tightened each time another well-meaning adult posed these questions, my shoulders instinctively rising toward my ears as if I could physically shield myself from the weight of unmade decisions. Ironically, making no decision seemed like the best decision at the time. Why didn't I know what I wanted to do after high school? Why couldn't I see a clear path forward, when everyone else seemed to have their route mapped out with such certainty?

All I knew with any clarity was that I loved dance and I loved understanding people. The studio floor beneath my feet and the mirror reflecting my movements was where I felt most myself, most connected, most alive. The meditative focus that comes with perfecting a single turn grounded me when everything else felt uncertain. I was fascinated by human behavior and connection, leaning me toward fields like psychology and sociology. How these interests might translate into a viable future remained foggy.

My parents encouraged me to apply to college gently but persistently. My mother would leave college brochures on my desk, the questioning glance from my father across the dinner table though loving, sent electricity through my nervous system like a low-grade current. These were somewhat forceful directives and consistent reminders that time was of the essence. Their concern carried the unmistakable scent of love mixed with worry; a parental perfume I'd known all my life. Meanwhile, I had no desire to even open a college brochure, each glossy pamphlet feeling like another reminder of my directionless state.

Divine guidance often appears through unlikely messengers. For me, it was my ballet teacher who mentioned her master's in dance program at the University at Buffalo. During one of our private lessons she said, "You know, Gina, you can major in dance at a university level."

This was something I had never considered. My heart rate quickened, my spine straightened, as if my body recognized this truth before my mind fully processed it. The idea that dance could be more than an extracurricular activity and become the actual focus of my higher education lifted my spirit.

I rushed home that evening, bubbling with newfound enthusiasm. The car keys jingled in my hand as I burst through our front door, always unlocked back then. The familiar scent of pizza wafted from the kitchen. "Mom, Dad, my ballet teacher told me I could major in dance! I think this is something I could actually do!" The excitement in my voice almost masked my underlying relief. Finally, I had a potential path that resonated with my heart.

Their responses did not mirror my enthusiasm. They held a parental pause that communicated volumes without words, their expressions a mixture of concern and calculation. As I sensed their hesitation, the kitchen light seemed to dim slightly. My father, a successful entrepreneur with a keen eye for viable business opportunities, seemed particularly hesitant about how dance could translate to future stability, his brow furrowing in that familiar way that indicated mental calculations were happening.

Well, if there was one thing my father taught me well, it was that in order to convince someone about your next step, you may have to bring in reinforcements and give a sales pitch. I thought up a strategy and approached my ballet teacher, asking if she would help my parents understand the legitimacy of this educational path. With her agreement, we arranged a meeting at the University at Buffalo to learn about the dance major together as a family.

The university campus felt both intimidating and exhilarating as we walked the pathways between buildings. The sound of our footsteps on the concrete paths, the distant laughter of students, and the rustle of wind through emerging leaves created a symphony of possibility that resonated in my chest.

Sitting in the department office, listening to professors describe the curriculum, I felt something click into place. It was not the dramatic revelation of movies, but a quiet, steady alignment. The office chair beneath me suddenly felt perfect, as if it had been waiting for me all along. The program was well structured and comprehensive, balancing technical training with theoretical knowledge and practical skills beyond just performance. For the first time, I could envision myself in this next chapter. This was a step I could take and honestly, it was the only clear step visible to me at that moment. Sometimes when choices are limited, making decisions becomes surprisingly simple.

The drive home in our family caravan carried both tension and curiosity. I sat in the back, heart racing with hope but also braced for rejection. Would my parents give me a chance to voice what I wanted, or would they simply deliver their verdict?

Then my father, with his entrepreneurial mind always calculating return on investment, broke the silence. "Gina," he began, his voice reflecting in the rearview mirror along with his eyes that briefly met mine, "here's what I like about the program." The fact that he was starting with positives rather than objections sent a surge of confidence through me.

"I like that you'll be learning skills that aren't just dance skills," he continued, the car slowing for a red light, the pause in movement emphasizing his words. "This curriculum seems to offer a well-rounded education that will teach you how to make money whether you end up dancing professionally or not. Therefore, I'm on board."

Those last three words unlocked something in my chest that had been tightly bound. The breath I hadn't realized I was holding released in a silent exhale, my shoulders dropping several inches from where they had been tensed around my ears. My father had seen something I hadn't fully articulated even to myself: that education in the arts develops transferable skills applicable across multiple career paths.

My mother simply smiled, with that smirk I knew so well as she replied, "Thank God." Her support came from the fact that I finally had decided to move forward.

I applied, auditioned, and was accepted to the University at Buffalo dance program notably late in the application cycle, a reminder that divine timing operates on its own schedule, not institutional deadlines. I started my freshman year in the governor's dorm, shared with other dance majors on the same dance scholarship I was on. The cinder block walls, painted an institutional burnt red, the narrow twin bunk beds, the communal bathroom with its perpetually wet floors these stark elements transformed into the backdrop for profound friendships and growth. My curriculum included morning ballet classes, modern and jazz, plus other artistic choices in a schedule that felt like a dream manifested: getting college credit for what I loved most in the world.

Freshman year brought the nervous excitement of new beginnings, but it was sophomore year that brought the knowledge of what artistic step I wanted to take. The realization came with a solo piece I prepared for my jazz class with Mr. Tom. A singular moment of recognition, as clear as the indent I had noticed on my right side years earlier, revealed what I truly wanted: to be a performer, to get paid to dance, to share the language of movement from stages rather than classrooms. My pulse quickened, not with anxiety but with recognition; this was where I belonged, this was what I wanted to pursue.

This heart-centered knowingness led to my next years at college feeling purposeful and fulfilling, even through the late nights of writing my thesis. Just as my father had predicted, I was developing versatility that would translate across departments and disciplines within the performing arts world, and I was going all in. The versatile curriculum covered dance technique across various styles. I learned choreography, K-12 teaching methods, dance history, and technical production skills including lighting, sound, and makeup.

Amongst all these wonderful classes, friendships and my artistic skills were growing. Toward the end of my junior year, something unexpected happened, a nudge to potentially graduate early. This restlessness wasn't something I could immediately explain, but it felt significant enough to discuss with Mr. Tom, the department chair and UB Dance Director, who had become a trusted mentor. Mr. Tom was as wise as an old dancing soul, his spirit and intuition always inspiring. I knew he would never tell me what to do but provide words of wisdom that would guide me well.

"Gina," he said after listening carefully to my thoughts, his hands forming a steeple beneath his chin, "I hear you. Like most students becoming seniors, you can get senioritis. It's normal. But I want to ask you why? You don't have to answer me right now, just sit with the question and tune into what is really making you want to graduate early." Most profoundly, our meeting ended with a last unexpected comment that gave me comfort and allowed me to make the decision about my potential early departure from college free from anxiety. My mentor's unforeseen comment was, "Gina, I will support you in whatever decision you choose."

His words weren't directive but invitational, creating space for my own wisdom to emerge rather than imposing his. I took his suggestion and found myself at Baird Point, a beautiful spot on campus where the rustling leaves and lapping water had often provided the backdrop for my deepest reflections. Sitting on a ledge, watching light dance across the water's surface, I finally heard what I now recognize as a divine whisper: "Be patient Gina, you're almost there."

Like a heavy winter coat being lifted off when snow disappears, I felt a lightness in choosing to stay and trust that what seemed like an arbitrary timeframe might actually be perfectly orchestrated for my personal and professional development. What had initially felt like a progressive nudge to graduate early revealed itself, through quiet reflection, to be the impatient part of me wanting to be ahead. The wisdom that emerged was profound: Five steps ahead isn't going to get me where I'm supposed to be, but where I want to be. There's a significant difference between those destinations.

My subsequent senior year was both challenging and transformational. My body went through unexpected changes, my dancing evolved in ways I couldn't have anticipated, and auditions began to yield promising results. I received enough positive feedback to validate my sophomore year revelation about performing. The rhythm of campus life morning technique classes, afternoon theory, evening rehearsals became a container for transformation beyond technique.

The simple gesture of choosing to stay taught me something, that senior year that I would have missed if I had graduated early: The return on investment isn't always measured in dollars. Sometimes it comes in skills developed, time well spent, knowledge acquired, or wisdom absorbed. Some investments aren't transactional but transformational, and my college experience transformed me not just physically but mentally, emotionally, and spiritually. My body became not just a tool for performance but a vessel for understanding, while my mind expanded beyond technique to encompass the profound human history of movement as communication. My father had been correct about the value of my education.

My graduation ceremony at the University at Buffalo held a magic that transcended the pomp and circumstance. Beyond the cap and gown, beyond the certificate naming my degree, I felt the profound completion of one cycle and the beginning of another. The weight of the tassel as I moved it from right to left, the subtle scent of new paper and ink on my diploma, the warmth of handshakes and hugs from faculty who had become family these sensory memories sealed the significance of the moment.

One of the most significant moments of all was the conversation with Mr. Tom. Mr. Tom saw beyond my technique to the essence of who I was becoming. He encouraged me when doubt clouded my vision, inspired me through his magnificent teaching methods, celebrated movement not just as an art form but as a way of being in the world, and, perhaps most significantly, acknowledged and invited my spiritual connection into our conversations about dance. His voice held a particular resonance that seemed to penetrate beyond my ears to reach something deeper, as if his words were tuning my very being to a higher frequency. This mentorship was something I could never have placed a monetary value on, and the relationship that continues to this day. Mr. Tom became more than an instructor; he became a touchstone I could return to throughout my professional journey, someone who would answer emails, meet for coffee, engage with questions, and offer perspective shaped by decades of experience in the field.

Looking back on those four years, I recognized that I had received exactly the education I needed to move forward, though I couldn't have articulated those needs when I first began. The dance major that once seemed like "the only option" had revealed itself to be precisely the most present path. Sometimes when we can't see the entire staircase, having faith in the next step is enough.

REVIVING THE SPIRIT

Reminders

Faith lives in the next true step: When the entire path isn't visible, divine guidance often reveals only the next stepping stone. Having faith doesn't mean seeing the entire journey mapped out; it means trusting that the single step you can see right now is enough to begin. My dance major wasn't my entire future revealed, but it was the exact next move that opened doors I couldn't have anticipated.

Divine wisdom often speaks through resistance: What feels like a challenge or unnecessary difficulty may actually be spiritual preparation for future gifts. Sometimes the very things we resist contain the seeds of our later liberation.

True investment is transformational, not just transactional: The greatest returns on investment can't be calculated on spreadsheets. My father initially looked for practical value in my dance education, but what I received transcended measurable outcomes: mentorship that shaped my character, and insights that continue to unfold decades later. The divine economy operates by different metrics than worldly accounting.

STEPS

🧴 **Lipstick:** "I trust the step I can see." Think of one small next step you can take toward something that calls to your heart, even if you can't see where it ultimately leads.

◉ **Lashes:** Look back at something you once resisted that later proved valuable. Perhaps it was a class you didn't want to take, a challenge you tried to avoid, or advice you initially rejected. What future gifts are your current resistances preparing you for?

✦ **God:** The divine often guides through human messengers, like my ballet teacher who introduced the possibility of a dance major, and Mr. Tom, who offered his unconditional support. Create a "Divine Suggestions" list in your journal or phone, writing down these divine messages without judgment.

PRAYER

Trusting the Next True Step

Divine Guide of My Journey,

Help me trust the single step I can see. Grant me courage to move forward in faith, embracing inner wisdom one authentic movement at a time.

Remind me that Your light doesn't illuminate the entire staircase but shines just enough for my next placement. In fog and uncertainty, help me listen deeply for inner guidance, trust fully in the timing presented, step boldly toward truth.

Transform my need for complete clarity into the willingness to walk by faith. Show me that sometimes the most powerful prayer is saying "yes" to the unknown.

With ease, please, reveal my next true action in this present moment.

Amen.

DIVINE GPS

"Your life unfolds in divinely sequenced steps that rarely follow logical order. Trust that each step, even the painful ones, even the seemingly misdirected ones, is preparing you for what comes next in your unique journey." GP

From Vegas Lights to Christmas Nights
Age 22-27 | Las Vegas to New York City

The desert air of Las Vegas hit my face as I stepped off the plane, a stark contrast to the Buffalo humidity I'd grown accustomed to throughout my college years. Graduation was behind me, and with my BFA degree from the University at Buffalo tucked safely in my suitcase, alongside leotards and dance shoes, I felt that unmistakable divine nudge guiding me west. A year before graduation, I'd seen a show here that lit something inside me, a performance that made my spirit soar in ways I couldn't articulate. Something about those lights, that energy, those dancers had planted a seed that grew into a certainty: this desert city was my next purpose step.

My senior semester, I'd flown to Las Vegas and auditioned for that very show, making it to the final round only to hear those dreaded words: "We'll let you know." A month before graduation, filled with that particular mix of hope and impatience that defined my early twenties, I called the casting director directly.

"Hey, it's Gina Pero," I said, trying to sound casual while my heart raced. "I'm about to graduate from college and I was wondering if I got the job."

His voice held a note of genuine regret. "I'm sorry, Gina. We loved you, however we have hired what we needed at this time. " "That's fine," I replied, the words automatic. Disappointment settled in my stomach like a stone.

Yet something inside me, that same intuitive pull that had always guided my biggest decisions, still urged me toward the West Coast. It wasn't logic; it was something deeper. The fear of not following my soul's calling was far greater than the fear of moving to a city without a guaranteed job. So I phoned a friend, confirmed I'd have a place to stay, and took the leap.

Landing in Vegas felt both terrifying and exactly right. The sensory overload of the Strip was overwhelming yet somehow energizing: lights flashing in patterns designed to captivate, slot machines creating their distinctive symphony, the particular blend of perfume, cigarette smoke, and recirculated air that defines casino spaces. This city, built on dreams and risk-taking, seemed to mirror the gamble I was taking with my own future.

Almost immediately, I booked my first gig, a one-time event where I was paid to dance. Success tasted sweet, validating my decision to come here. But while in the dressing room that night, surrounded by sequins and stage makeup, I overheard dancers talking about how the show I'd originally auditioned for, my dream show, was closing in two weeks.

Sitting before the mirror, watching my face fall at this news, I felt a moment of doubt creep in. Had I moved across the country for nothing? But at twenty-two, my faith was as boundless as my energy. My confidence, a precious combination of youth and hard-earned skill, remained unshaken. Something else would open up. It had to.

I went to see the final performance of my dream show, allowing myself to feel both the disappointment and the appreciation for what had brought me here. Sitting in the audience, the theater lights dimming around me, I offered up a silent prayer: "God, show me the plan for my life, teach me what I need to know, I'm in Las Vegas and I know something brought me here."

Divine timing has a fascinating way of revealing itself. I auditioned for another show called *Airplay* and got it. Walking into my first rehearsal, I discovered that almost all the dancers were from the show that had just closed, the very one I'd originally wanted to join. Confirmation blazed through me like stage lights: This was exactly where I was supposed to be.

The show schedule was intense seven performances daily, though we rotated cast members to make it manageable. The director's enthusiasm, the musicians' talent, and the other dancers' professionalism created the perfect environment for beginning my professional career. I learned invaluable lessons about hair and makeup, about pacing myself through multiple performances, and about projecting energy to the back row without sacrificing technique. This was my next step in dance, and I embraced every moment of it.

Las Vegas became my playground and classroom. I booked modeling jobs, networked constantly, met incredible artists, and even traveled internationally to perform in China and Japan. My father's entrepreneurial teachings proved invaluable as I navigated the business side of being a professional dancer, managing my own finances, marketing myself, and building a reputation for reliability and skill.

Yet despite the excitement and success, something inside me remained restless. It wasn't the fear of missing out that plagues so many young adults, but rather the fear of not fully answering my calling. While performing at an event, gold sequins catching the light with each movement, questions began dancing through my mind: What would it be like to go to New York City? What would it be like to experience New York as a dancer?

The thought kept returning, persistent as a melody you can't shake. "If you can make it there, you can make it anywhere," the famous lyrics promised. So once again, I followed my heart's guidance and called my friend Jason.

"I want to come to New York and just see if I like it," I told him. "Do you mind if I stay with you?"

Jason, both a dear friend and respected teacher, welcomed me without hesitation. Within weeks, I was walking the streets of Manhattan, the energy of the city vibrating through the concrete into my dancer's bones. The air felt different here, charged with urgency and possibility, carrying the distinct blend of street vendor food, car exhaust, and that indefinable New York scent that somehow smells like opportunity.

During my visit, a "random" audition appeared, one for a dance agency. Divine timing again. I decided to go, entering a room packed with dancers from everywhere, their bodies tense with the particular anticipation unique to auditions. By incredible synchronicity, I bumped into a college friend who was assisting at the audition.

The fire inside me blazed bright that day. I was driven not just by ambition but by something purer, the desire to fully express who I was created to be through movement. Every combination, every piece of choreography felt right in my body. I left that audition feeling renewed in my identity as a dancer, my purpose reaffirmed through sweat and musicality and the particular joy of dancing alongside others equally committed to this art.

The very next day, on my flight back to Las Vegas, a voicemail was left on my phone: "Gina, we would love to have you as part of our agency."

I knew enough about the industry to understand that a New York dance agent wouldn't represent someone living across the country. So when I called back, words emerged from my mouth that surprised even me: "I'm in Las Vegas doing a gig, but I'll be moving to New York City in March."

After hanging up, reality hit me. Did I just commit to moving across the country? No job guarantees. No place to stay. An apartment in Las Vegas to deal with. Yet I recognized that familiar sensation my grandmother had taught me to identify, the Holy Spirit moving through us in key moments. No logical thinking would have produced those words; they came from somewhere deeper.

Everything flowed with remarkable ease: finding storage for my things, breaking my lease, making arrangements. This smoothness confirmed I was on the right path. When things are in flow, when they feel easy despite their complexity, I've learned that's often a sign of divine alignment. God was present. My angels were surrounding me. This was my next purpose step.

I called Jason again, asking if his offer of a place to stay was still open. His generous "yes" allowed me to pack just two suitcases and embark on this new chapter. On the plane ride to New York, one set of fears dissolved while others emerged. The fear of not following my soul's purpose was replaced by more practical anxieties: Am I good enough? How will I make money? How will I find my own place?

But stepping onto New York pavement, breathing in that distinctive city air, I knew. This was exactly where I needed to be, and that knowledge was enough to take my next step.

The New York dance scene embraced me with its particular intensity. Classes at Steps on Broadway and

Broadway Dance Center, where the floors held the history of countless dancers before me. Auditions where the tension in the room was thick enough to touch. Calls from my new agent, each one a potential opportunity. I wasn't just following a dream I'd created; I was answering a calling that felt imprinted on my soul.

After seeing the Radio City Rockettes perform, their precision and synchronicity creating patterns that seemed almost mathematically perfect, I was encouraged to audition the following year. The audition was unlike anything I'd experienced, a thousand dancers wrapped around Radio City Music Hall, the line snaking through the streets of Manhattan. Standing there in my sunglasses with a side-swept ponytail, I felt that familiar fire ignite.

The audition itself was pressure in its purest form. Everything had to be perfect. Teachers counted sharply, "Five, six, seven, eight!" their voices carrying the weight of decades of tradition. The dancers around me were extraordinary, their technique flawless, their performance quality magnetic. This was precision dance at its finest, and the standards were impossibly high.

I made it through the first day and advanced to the second. That night, lying in bed with muscles aching from maintaining the Rockettes' distinctive posture, I had a conversation with God that came straight from my competitive spirit: "This was the hardest audition of my entire life. I will crush it tomorrow. I am going in there and I will $#@% crush it."

The next day, I channeled my inner athlete, the basketball player taught by my father to fight until the final buzzer. The Rocky Balboa "Eye of the Tiger" mentality had gotten me through tough moments before. This wasn't just dance; this was spiritual warfare for my dream.

After the audition ended, I was measured for potential costumes (a promising sign). Then, the waiting began.

The particular torture of audition limbo settled in as I tried to be present in daily life while constantly checking my phone, wondering if today would be the day my future changed.

It was the beginning of July, and sunlight reflected off Manhattan skyscrapers as I crossed a street to assist Jason at a convention, when my phone rang. I had made it: I was cast in the Radio City Music Hall Christmas Spectacular tour. And the location of my first performance? Shea's Buffalo, the very theater where my grandmother had first taken me as a child, the place where my vision of becoming a dancer was born. I was going home, not just to my hometown but to the origin of my dream. I was going to be in the famous kickline near the place where it all began.

In that moment, I understood something profound about divine guidance. Sometimes God brings us places not just for our own dreams but for a higher purpose that includes others. My journey from Buffalo to Las Vegas to New York and back to Buffalo again wasn't random; it was a perfectly choreographed divine sequence.

Summer passed in a blur of conditioning and preparation. By the fall, I was packing my bags for Myrtle Beach, where rehearsals would be held. Looking back at my path, from the desire to experience Las Vegas to the burning need to try New York, coupled with the fear of not honoring my purpose, I could see how each step had led precisely to this moment. It was not the path I would have consciously designed, but exactly the journey my spirit needed.

What no one saw behind the achievement were the personal struggles running parallel to this professional triumph. My cousin had been diagnosed with leukemia and passed away in December 2007, just as my Rockette journey was beginning. Our family was navigating grief while I was learning kicklines. Simultaneously, I was trapped in a unhealthy relationship, and I didn't yet know how to get out of it.

The contrast between public success and private pain was stark. Most of my family and friends didn't know what was happening behind the scenes in my personal life, just as I barely recognized the depth of what was occurring in my family's life.

During this painful period, Lourdes entered the story like an angel in human form. I had met her when I was seventeen, when she asked me a question no one had ever posed before: "What do you dream? Dream big." Though technically my aunt's best friend, Lourdes and I had developed a profound connection that sometimes felt like we had known each other in previous lives.

She was everything I aspired to be: gentle yet powerful, compassionate yet direct, successful yet humble. A Cuban entrepreneur who ran her own company, she taught me about business, fashion, and presence. Her intuition was legendary; she sensed things before they happened, spoke truths that manifested, and saw in me potential I couldn't yet recognize in myself.

While we were home celebrating my cousin's life, one year prior to my start with the Rockettes, Lourdes quietly handed me a check for $2,500, saying simply, "You know exactly what you need to do with this." And I did. That money allowed me to return to Las Vegas and get my own apartment. Without hesitation or doubt, I made the change immediately upon landing, not even returning to my previous residence.

Life unfolds in steps that rarely follow the logical sequence our minds want to create. Sometimes we question the order, wanting to jump ahead to step five when we're still learning the lessons of step one. In the kickline, being on the wrong step meant getting a note from the director; in life, it means missing the gifts each phase is designed to give us.

My first season with the Rockettes was a blessing beyond description. The rehearsal process was the most challenging work I'd ever done, demanding a level of precision and stamina that pushed me to my absolute limits. Then opening night arrived, with sixty family members in the audience waiting for the curtain to rise.

Kneeling in my reindeer pose backstage, the familiar scent of theater dust and makeup filling my nostrils, I felt tears streaming down my cheeks. My lipstick and lashes were carefully applied, but in that moment, I felt God's presence more clearly than the costume on my body. This performance wasn't about me or my achievement; it was about giving back to everyone who had supported me, believed in me, and loved me through every step of the journey.

As the curtain rose and my family cheered from the audience, I moved into my first sharp arm movement with the awareness that my cousin's spirit was with us too. It wasn't just a performance; it was a shared spiritual experience, a moment of collective joy amid grief.

The show closed with "Hark the Herald Angels Sing," my cousin's favorite song. As the music played, I looked upward, knowing somehow that he had orchestrated this convergence of events: my family together, celebrating Christmas, finding magic and purpose and community in the midst of loss. I was coming home not just physically but spiritually, home to who I was becoming, home to why I was here at this moment, and home to the community of people that had supported me through all my childhood years.

This I knew was the divine GPS that was already calculating and preparing my path, guiding me towards my next purpose step. And I knew with certainty my inner divine GPS would continue to recalculate my path based on where my soul truly needed to go.

REVIVING THE SPIRIT

Reminders

Trust the divine choreography: My path from Buffalo to Las Vegas to New York and back to Buffalo wasn't random but perfectly sequenced for my growth. What seems like detours are often divine redirections toward something better aligned with your purpose. The sequence of your life rarely makes logical sense until you look backward and see the perfect timing of each step.

Honor your soul's calling: The fear of not following your purpose is more significant than the fear of taking risks. When something resonates in your soul, whether it's moving across the country or changing careers, that persistent inner knowing is often divine guidance. My impulsive declaration about moving to New York came from something deeper than logic; it was my spirit recognizing its path before my mind could catch up.

Trust your internal divine GPS: When the path seems to lead away from your dreams, remember that divine navigation often takes unexpected routes to reach your true destination. What looks like a detour may be the most direct path to your purpose. Trust that the same guidance system that got you this far knows exactly where you need to go next.

STEPS

🔺 Lipstick: What persistent inner nudge have you been ignoring because it seems impractical or risky? Take that step with the same bold confidence you apply lipstick before an important event with intention, precision, and a belief in your own beauty.

◉ Lashes: Look around for the Lourdes figures in your life, those people who see your potential more clearly than you do. Who has asked about your dreams lately? Who has offered help that seemed to come at exactly the right moment?

✦ God: Create your own "reindeer pose" moment, a time of stillness before taking your next big step. Kneel or sit in meditation, acknowledging both your fears and your dreams. Ask: "Show me the plan for my life, teach me what I need to know." Then listen for guidance that might come as a thought, memory, or seemingly random opportunity. Remember that divine purposes often extend beyond personal achievement to touch others in ways we cannot foresee.

PRAYER

For Next Purpose Steps

Divine Choreographer,

Grant me wisdom to recognize divine timing, understanding that closed doors are often redirections toward something better aligned with who I'm becoming.

Give me courage when my heart whispers paths my logical mind cannot comprehend. When words spring from my mouth surprising even me, let me recognize Your spirit moving.

Open my eyes to human angels You've placed in my path. In moments of impatience, remind me each step has its timing and purpose. Help me honor the sequence You've designed.

With ease, please, guide me forward into Your perfect plan.

Amen.

THE DIVINE KNOCKOUT

"What appears to be knocking you down may actually be lifting you toward your true calling. Your greatest setbacks often contain the seeds of your most meaningful redirection, if you're willing to see divine intention in unexpected packaging." GP

Finding Purpose Beyond the Spotlight
Age 29-30 | Dallas, Atlanta, and New York

Every journey has its pivotal moment, the turning point where everything that came before suddenly makes sense and everything that follows takes on new purpose. For me, that moment came in the most unexpected and dramatic way, bringing together all the threads of my story into a divine tapestry I never could have designed myself.

Season two found me on tour again with the Radio City Rockettes, this time in Dallas and Atlanta. I was assigned the same position: stage right end girl, the dancer all the way on the left if you're facing the stage. Being less tall (we never used the word "short" in the

Rockettes), I was placed at the end, but this position carried extra responsibility. As the line captain, I set the mark that everyone else followed through peripheral vision. Every toe placement had to be precise, guided by the stage grid that mapped our movements with mathematical accuracy.

This was the culmination of everything I'd been working toward since those early days in the studio with my curved spine, since the moment Miss Lisa told me she believed in me, since the disappointments and triumphs that had led me to this prestigious position. By all external measures, I had "made it." I should have been fulfilled, satisfied, and complete.

Yet beneath the precision, the rhinestones, and the famous kickline, the question that had followed me throughout my journey whispered more insistently: Was this truly my purpose?

I felt less pressure this second season but still strove for excellence in every performance. With seventeen shows a week and three-hundred kicks per show, the physical demands remained intense. But something was shifting within me, a growing awareness, a deeper questioning that surfaced, particularly during the Nativity scene one show night.

Those twelve minutes when the Rockettes stood as gift bearers while live animals and actors portrayed the Christmas story became my sacred time. Night after night, as the familiar scene unfolded, I entered into conversations with God. One particular evening, standing there in my costume while the audience watched Mary and Joseph, I had what people often call a "come to Jesus moment" a raw, honest prayer that arose from depths I hadn't fully acknowledged:

God, I am not happy. I know I should be this is what dancers dream of but my body hurts. I'm grateful, yet not grateful. I don't think this is my purpose and in this moment, I have to be honest. There's something greater for me, and I know it, yet I don't know what it is. I am struggling. So many dancers want this position, and yet something feels off. I need your help and guidance.

The words raced through my mind, as I stood perfectly still, maintaining the precise posture required of a Rockette while my inner world trembled with vulnerability. This wasn't the prayer of a dancer uncertain about her talents, as I had been when Miss Lisa's four words saved my dancing journey. This wasn't the confusion of a high school senior unsure which college path to take.

This was something deeper: the recognition that even at the pinnacle of my dancing career, something essential was missing. All the physical challenges I'd overcome with my scoliosis, all the wobbles I'd transformed into information rather than failure, all the steps I'd taken, trusting the unfolding path, had led me here, to this moment of profound honesty on a stage representing the very birth of divine purpose in human form.

Have you ever found yourself in a position others would envy, yet known deep within that something wasn't aligned? Have you ever felt the disconnect between external success and internal fulfillment? That night, standing in a scene about divine birth, I was experiencing my own labor pains, the uncomfortable stretching that precedes new life.

The very next day, during intermission, I was walking backstage to take my position for the "Christmas in New York" number. We wore beautiful red skirts with white fur trim and matching Santa hats adorned with red rhinestones the epitome of Christmas glamour. As I moved through the backstage area, suddenly and without warning, a fist connected with my chin. My neck snapped back, and the world went dark.

A dancer next to me managed to catch me before I hit the floor completely, but I was already unconscious on the way down. Having recently read Dr. Jill Bolte Taylor's *My Stroke of Insight* and developed an interest in neuroscience, I had just enough awareness to understand what was happening. Though unconscious, a part of me recognized that my body was convulsing, legs kicking involuntarily. I could hear voices saying, "Stop kicking, relax," but couldn't make the connection between understanding these commands and getting my body to obey them.

Tingling sensations spread through my jaw, eyes, and nose. I felt as though my eyes were rolling back, as if my teeth might fall out sensations that were probably the result of disrupted neural pathways. When one of our managers gently grabbed my hand, something released. My body relaxed, and I sat up, disoriented but conscious.

My first words upon regaining consciousness? "Okay, I'll go get my ragdoll costume on and I'll be right back." At twenty-nine years old, I was so conditioned to pushing through pain, so afraid of letting others down, so identified with my role as a performer, that even a serious injury couldn't override this programming. My immediate instinct was to continue, to ignore the warning signals my body was desperately sending.

In that moment, I embodied everything I had been through on my journey: the determined girl who danced despite her scoliosis, the persistent student who kept balancing after countless wobbles, the professional who moved to Las Vegas and then New York in pursuit of her dreams, the performer who found divinity in unexpected temples while touring Japan. But this time, the universe had a more dramatic intervention planned than Miss Lisa's gentle words or the sacred fire in Tokyo.

Of course, they took me to the emergency room instead. On the way, I tried texting a friend but couldn't form coherent sentences, a frightening indicator of cognitive impact. At the hospital, as my manager explained to medical staff that I was normally "organized and sharp, the line captain," I stood in the waiting room, eyes looking upwards, watching a television program that was honoring everyday heroes making remarkable impacts in the world. I mean, was this God speaking to me about my purpose or what?

The synchronicity wasn't lost on me, even in my compromised state. The prayer from the previous night about finding my greater purpose, followed by this concussion, followed by witnessing stories of meaningful impact beyond performance ... It felt like divine choreography, each element positioned with intention. This was the culmination of everything the universe had been trying to tell me through gentler messages I had missed or misinterpreted.

This injury occurred around the time the National Football League was implementing new concussion protocols, requiring players to sit out for fourteen days after a head injury. Radio City had no such policy at the time, making me something of a guinea pig for their approach to concussion management. Two friends had to sleep in my room, waking me throughout the night to ask orientation questions and monitor my condition.

Now I faced a new reality: If I wanted to heal, I had to listen to my body rather than override it. Fear still coursed through me, fear that if I didn't quickly return to the show, they wouldn't hire me again; fear that my career was over; fear of losing the identity I'd worked so hard to build. But beneath that fear lay a deeper truth: Gina's soul and Gina's body were not winning in this scenario. Something had to change.

This became the first time in my life where I had to make a decision that truly put my wellbeing first. I had to acknowledge that this body and brain needed to be the most valuable players in my life if I wanted to continue living my dreams in any capacity. It was a radical shift in perspective, especially in an environment where I didn't see others honoring their bodies, where pushing through injury was the norm rather than the exception.

Recovery came in increments. I would do ten minutes of exercise and, if no symptoms appeared, I could try fifteen minutes the next day. If fifteen minutes went well, perhaps twenty minutes would follow. This methodical, patient approach felt foreign to someone accustomed to pushing boundaries, but it was the only path forward.

The concussion forced me to employ everything I'd learned throughout my journey, from the patience required while overcoming scoliosis to the perseverance that kept me dancing after countless rejections, from the trust in divine timing I'd discovered within that temple in Tokyo. All these experiences had been preparing me for this moment of profound surrender and transformation.

Though I never returned to perform that season, the concussion became an unexpected answer to my prayer in the Nativity scene. God had quite literally knocked me out to lift me up, showing me my purpose through what initially seemed like a setback. The journey wasn't easy. I hadn't specified "with ease, please" in my prayer (a clause I now recommend adding to all divine requests!) but it was transformative.

This injury led me toward holistic health practices that workers' compensation wouldn't cover, from cranial sacral therapy to biofeedback, reiki, homeopathy, and energy medicine. Intuitively, I knew these approaches would help me really heal. I was not interested in a temporary fix or mask at this time, so I focused on things that promised a good return on investment. I invested significant personal resources in a whole-person approach, knowing that these services would help me to live fully moving forward. I knew that in order for my body to heal, I also had to heal my emotions, thoughts, and spirit.

I remember receiving a phone call from my homeopath one day. She never called, so I answered. As it turned out, her call came at the perfect time: I was headed out the door, attempting to go back to the show, which I told her. She said, "Gina, how are you feeling?" I said I was okay but looking in the mirror, it was clear I was not. She asked, "Do you have a headache?" I said, "Yes." And then she said, "Well then, you can call your director and let them know you will not be going in." I hung up the phone with defeat and made one of the most difficult calls of my life.

Why did I feel such shame and failure calling out of the show? Why did being honest about a headache feel like I was quitting? I had so much to heal beyond the physical. In that moment, I knew a little bit more about what needed to be healed on this journey and God must have known that I was asking for purpose, that this personal healing journey was the next step. While I was frightened and ashamed, wondering whether I could do this or not, something greater than myself was taking the lead. The real line captain had shown up and instead of "guiding right," as we say in the kickline, I was guiding myself toward the light.

What appeared as a career-threatening injury became the redirection toward my true calling. The concussion didn't end my story; it began a new chapter one where

I could help others honor their bodies and listen to divine guidance, finding purpose beyond performance. Of course, I had to become the student before I could become the teacher.

The stage had been my world, but now the world became my stage for a different kind of dance, one of healing, teaching, and living in the highest and best alignment with divine purpose.

The journey that followed, became my life's greatest teacher, though not an easy one. For the first time, I was forced to truly honor my body's signals. Any symptom, headache, tingling, eye dilation, was a sign to stop all activity and start over. Quitting had never been in my vocabulary as a dancer, so listening to the headaches didn't stop me; the pain didn't stop me; even the fear of missing opportunities didn't stop me. Remember, I had asked for this: I asked God to show me my purpose, and I was honest about my own feelings and sense of where I was. Even though we think we should be grateful for something, we can still be grateful and admit we don't like something anymore. What came to me was the equivalent of "Ask and you shall receive." My Nana used to say be careful what you ask for now I was experiencing that firsthand.

Looking back, I understand now the profound truth in those ancient words: "Ask and you shall receive." The universe had delivered precisely what I'd requested, clarity about my purpose, though the package it came in was far from what I would have chosen. My concussion wasn't just an accident; it was a divine appointment, a cosmic response to my honest prayer.

The divine knockout became my greatest blessing, though disguised as my greatest setback. That single moment of impact during my second season redirected my entire life trajectory, though I wouldn't fully understand this until later.

I returned for a third season, dancing with new awareness, my body healed, but my spirit permanently shifted. Throughout that final season, the question of purpose that had haunted me during the Nativity scene continued to evolve. I was no longer asking if this was my purpose, I knew it was for a period of time, and it was time to move on.

It was after that third season where my purpose continued to crystallize, and I pursued my coaching certification through the International Coaching Federation. The concussion hadn't just ended one chapter; it had begun revealing the next one. Dancing had been my first language, but coaching was becoming my second, and my way of helping others find their own voice, their own movement, and their own divine purpose." The program offered an in depth "Coaching for Transformation," tagline, that gifted me with techniques and tools my inner stage chose to learn. Just like the choreography of a staged routine, these months were spent on life choreography that I knew I was ready for. It was as if the divine knockout was really stretching me into divine alignment, a new kind of a dance, yet the most profound style.

This is the mysterious paradox of divine guidance: Sometimes what knocks us down is exactly what lifts us up. Sometimes being removed from everything familiar is the only way we can discover what we're truly meant to do. Sometimes the very thing we resist becomes the doorway to our greatest gifts.

Had my prayer in the Nativity scene been more specific, "Show me my purpose, with ease please," perhaps the pathway would have been gentler. But would I have listened? Would I have made such a radical shift without such a dramatic intervention? Sometimes the universe knows exactly what intensity level is required to break through our conditioning and resistance.

The divine knockout isn't meant to end your story, it's meant to begin the chapter you were always destined to live.

And remember to add "with ease, please" to your deepest prayers. The universe is listening more attentively than you know.

REVIVING THE SPIRIT

Reminders

Pay attention to recurring messages: When the same suggestion, idea, or invitation appears repeatedly in your life, pay attention it's rarely a coincidence. The universe often sends multiple confirmations before major redirections, knowing our human tendency to dismiss singular instances as random.

Honest prayer precedes transformation: The most powerful prayers aren't polished or perfect, they're raw expressions of your true condition. When I stood in that Nativity scene confessing my unhappiness in a position others envied, I opened a channel for divine intervention. God responds most powerfully not to our pretenses of having it all together but to our honest acknowledgment of misalignment and need for guidance.

Be specific in your divine requests: When you pray for guidance or change, include how you'd like it to arrive. Adding "with ease, please" to your prayers acknowledges that you're open to divine redirection without unnecessary suffering. The universe responds to clarity and specificity, so be mindful about what you're truly asking for.

STEPS

💄 Lipstick: "I welcome divine redirection with grace and ease." Think of a current challenge or setback you're facing. Instead of seeing it as an obstacle, reframe it as a divine response to your deeper prayers.

👁 Lashes: Look back at pivotal moments when you were "knocked down" in some way, whether through illness, injury, loss, or unexpected change. For each situation, ask yourself: What door closed? What door opened? How did this redirection ultimately lead to growth or new possibilities?

✨ God: Create a "Divine Request" practice this week. Each night before sleep, formulate one clear, specific prayer about guidance, purpose, or transformation you're seeking. Always end with "with ease, please" as a reminder that divine alignment doesn't require suffering.

PRAYER

Divine Redirection

Master of Sacred Timing,

When my plans are interrupted, path diverted, dreams delayed or denied, help me see Your hand at work. Grant me humility to recognize that being knocked down may be lifting toward greater purpose.

When doors close, open my eyes to new doorways I hadn't noticed. Give me courage to follow divine detours, wisdom to recognize holy redirection, faith to trust Your choreography surpasses my imagination.

Help me understand that setbacks often contain seeds of meaningful redirection. Transform my disappointments into divine appointments, my obstacles into opportunities.

With ease, please, show me the gift within every challenge I face.

Amen

STARTING OVER

"Your discomfort isn't punishment, it's guidance. When you feel most vulnerable, stripped of familiar identities and achievements, you're actually closest to discovering your authentic purpose beyond all masks." GP

When Discomfort Leads to Divine Direction
Age 31-32 | Sardinia to Batavia, New York to Las Vegas

The recycled air of the airplane cabin felt heavy against my skin as we began our descent. My spirit had been revived during my time in Sardinia, leaving me feeling calm, peaceful, and centered throughout most of the long flight home. But as the pilot announced our approach to New York, fear began to rise up my back like cool water climbing a shore. After living abroad, I was returning to Batavia, my childhood home, without a plan, uncertain of what awaited me next.

Italy had transformed me. The cobblestone streets of Sardinia, the particular quality of Mediterranean light that makes everything look slightly golden, the unhurried pace of life where three-hour lunches were considered normal all of it had stripped away layers of American hustle and my achievement-driven identity. There, no one had cared about my resume or past accomplishments. People connected with the essence of who I was, not what I had done. The simpler lifestyle had revealed parts of myself I'd never known existed beneath the constant striving.

Now, at the age of thirty-two, I was moving back into my parents' attic. The very thought tightened my chest and quickened my breathing. In Italy, adult children commonly lived with parents well into their thirties, a cultural norm that felt natural in that context. But in America, this same arrangement carried the weight of failure, of regression, of dreams abandoned. I had no direction, no drive, no awareness, no sense of anything, really. For the first time in a long time, Gina Pero had no clear next step.

The attic room of my childhood home smelled of cedar and old books, familiar yet strange after so much time away. Dust particles danced in the slanted light from the small window that overlooked Trumbull Parkway. My suitcases sat unpacked in the corner, as if physically opening them would make this transition too real, too permanent. I heard the muffled sounds of my parents moving around downstairs, their voices and footsteps a soundtrack from an earlier chapter of my life.

I reached out to friends, seeking connection and perhaps direction. My dad offered his empty building as a potential dance studio, a generous gesture that sparked a flicker of possibility. I took ballet class from a dear friend who was teaching at Buffalo State University, my muscles remembering patterns my mind seemed to have forgotten. I was open to whatever might come next, but beneath that openness lay a profound misery that I couldn't shake.

My journal entries from this period reveal a darkness I hadn't experienced before. The pages filled with heavy ink and heavier words, each one weighted with disconnection not just from what I wanted to do but from who I was becoming. The mirror in my bathroom reflected a face I barely recognized, eyes dulled by what I later realized wasn't actually depression but a profound spiritual disorientation.

Some part of me had indeed died in Italy, the part that defined success through external validation and achievement. A year prior, I had been a Radio City Rockette, living in New York City, "making it" by all conventional standards. Now I found myself in a small town with nothing impressive to tell people about my current life. The contrast was jarring, like stepping off stage from blinding spotlights into complete darkness. I didn't like the way I felt living at home again. I didn't like the thoughts that circled my mind like hungry wolves. I didn't like where I was or who I seemed to have become. The sheets on my childhood bed felt simultaneously too familiar and completely uncomfortable against my skin.

Then, in the divine economy of growth, something showed up just when the discomfort became unbearable. Sitting on the front porch of my parents' home one evening, the wooden swing creaking beneath me as mosquitos began their nightly chorus, a realization washed over me like the sunset colors spreading across the sky: Why was I so uncomfortable sitting in the unknown? Why did I need something impressive to tell people I was doing? What was this discomfort really about?

The porch that had hosted countless family conversations, morning coffees, and teenage confidences now became the setting for a profound conversation with myself. As I looked out at the neighborhood that had shaped my earliest dreams, watching fireflies begin to appear against the darkening trees, the truth emerged with crystal clarity. The discomfort wasn't about lacking a plan, it was about being stripped down to just me, without the makeup, costumes, and spotlight—without the lipstick and lashes. The discomfort was about facing myself without the mask of achievement. The discomfort was feeling like I'd experienced a loss, because American society measures worth through visible success rather than inner growth.

Divine timing arrived in the form of a choreography invitation from a dear friend. Though unpaid, this opportunity to create and move again felt like water to parched earth. In the studio, the familiar scent of rosin and sweat welcoming me back, I found dance serving a new purpose. It wasn't about performing on stage or impressing an audience; it was simply about moving energy through my body, shifting from stagnation to flow. With each rehearsal, each stretch and turn and leap, something inside me began to loosen, like ice melting after a long winter.

What stops us from moving when movement is exactly what we need? What keeps us frozen in discomfort rather than dancing our way through it? These questions became my meditation as I worked through this challenging period, one day at a time, one step at a time.

Then, like a spotlight suddenly illuminating a darkened stage, an email appeared in my inbox: "You have two free tickets to a coaching conference in Los Angeles." I stared at the screen, the blue light reflecting on my face as I felt that familiar spark of knowing, the same certainty I'd experienced years ago when I knew I needed to move to New York City. This was another divine nudge, another next step appearing just when I needed it most.

The timing was complicated. For months, I'd been cleaning out my dad's building, installing mirrors, preparing to open my own dance studio. My father had invested time, energy, and resources into helping me build this new venture. How could I tell him that something else was calling to my spirit more loudly?

Walking down the stairs to have this conversation, each step creaking beneath my feet, I felt the weight of potential disappointment. The smell of my father's cooking filled the house, a mixture of tomato sauce and garlic that had always meant home. My father sat in his usual rocking chair, the evening news playing softly in the background.

"Dad?" I called, my voice betraying my nervousness. He looked up, his blue eyes meeting mine. "Yes, dear?" The words tumbled out, explaining about the coaching conference, the opportunity, the inexplicable pull I felt toward it. "I know we've been working on building this studio and you've been putting a lot of time and energy into helping me. But I just got this email offering two tickets to LA for this coaching conference, and I really want to go." I paused, feeling like that young girl asking for dance lessons all over again. "Would you be able to help pay for my flight?"

The silence that followed felt eternal, filled only with the subtle ticking of the mantel clock and my own heartbeat pounding in my ears. Then my father, his entrepreneurial eyes never leaving mine, said something that remains etched in my heart as a perfect example of unconditional love: "Gina, if this is something that is going to make you happy, then go, and I will help you pay for it."

He continued, wisdom flowing from a place of deep knowing: "I told you a while ago that I felt coaching was really a next step for you. I know you have what it takes to be a great coach."

Tears streamed down my face as we embraced, the familiar scent of his aftershave bringing comfort just as it had throughout my childhood. Here was love without condition, love that recognized the value of following inner light even when it meant changing course, love that saw beyond sunk costs to the ultimate investment in joy and purpose.

Soon I found myself on another plane, notebook in hand, pen ready, eager to absorb everything the Message to Millions conference had to offer. The anticipation that filled me created a buzzing energy, like the moment just before music begins and dancers take their opening positions. This felt right in a way that setting up a dance studio hadn't. While the studio hadn't felt wrong, it also hadn't aligned with my current evolution.

When we're in alignment with divine purpose, synchronicities appear like stepping stones across a stream. At the conference, I met extraordinary people whose paths seemed destined to cross mine. The teachings resonated deep in my body, not just my mind, creating that unmistakable feeling of "yes" that comes when truth is recognized. The motivational energy in the room fed something in me that had been starving, reconnecting me to purpose and possibility.

Throughout the conference, one question kept arising: "What's my next step?" Not the entire staircase, not the five-year plan, just the very next place to put my foot. The answer began to appear early one morning on the hotel treadmill, where I was doing my usual dance-inspired workout. Next to me, a man who exuded confidence and knowledge in the coaching industry matched my pace. Our conversation flowed as easily as our movements, and soon we were exchanging ideas and contact information.

"What do you think my next step could be?" I asked him during a coffee break later that day, the steam from our cups creating momentary veils between us.
"Well, I think you need a niche, Gina," he replied, stirring his coffee thoughtfully. "If you want to be a coach, what's your specialty?"
The word "niche" was new to me, but coincidentally, a speaker at the conference addressed exactly this topic that same afternoon. She explained that a niche was a specific focus area for coaching a particular group of people or specific set of challenges you help clients overcome. As she spoke, her words resonating through the conference hall, clarity struck me like a spotlight: finding my niche was my next step.

This speaker clearly knew her stuff, but her $10,000 coaching fee might as well have been a million dollars given the state of my bank account. How could I possibly work with her? The question hovered in my mind as I navigated the crowded conference hall during a break, the air conditioning raising goosebumps on my arms despite the California heat outside.

Then came what I call "the divine bump." Literally. As I was walking out the door, the same woman I had just seen on stage came walking in, and we crashed into each other.

"I'm so inspired by your speech," I gushed, words tumbling out before I could filter them. "I'm in awe of what you do, and I really know you're my next step. I don't know what that looks like, but I'm a dancer and ..."

"You're a dancer?" she interrupted, her eyes lighting up. "I love dance! I have an event in Las Vegas coming up."

Before my logical mind could catch up, the Holy Spirit was moving through me fast: "Well, don't you need an opening number?"

Her enthusiasm matched mine. "Of course! Is that something you can do?"

"Yes," I replied without hesitation, "I have a group called the Peroettes (using my last name as the brand of course) in Las Vegas." The words flowed from somewhere beyond conscious thought—I had no such group, but in that moment, possibility overrode practicality.

The exchange that followed felt like divine choreography: She offered free tickets to her workshop for me and "my dancers" in exchange for creating and performing an opening number for her Las Vegas event. What had seemed impossible moments before was now unfolding with miraculous ease.

Flying back from the conference, the California sunset painting the clouds in shades of pink and gold outside my window, excitement bubbled through me. I called friends in Las Vegas, secured a place to stay, and connected with dancers willing to perform in exchange for the workshop tickets. Within days, I was in a studio again, the mirror reflecting not just my movements but my renewed purpose as I created the opening number. Las Vegas, a city I never thought I'd return to, suddenly seemed to be calling me back for some higher purpose. Job opportunities appeared. Connections rekindled. Everything flowed with an ease that confirmed I was on my present path. The desert air, dry and electric with possibility, welcomed me back as if it had been waiting for my return.

The hardest part was telling my parents I was moving again. Flying home to have this conversation, watching the landscape change from desert to farmland below me, I rehearsed my words carefully. But when I arrived, something had visibly shifted in me, and my parents noticed it immediately. My smile reached my eyes again. My energy had transformed from stagnant to flowing. I was lit up in a way they hadn't seen since before Italy.

When I explained my plans, my father's response carried the weight of years of wisdom: "Gina, as you go back to Las Vegas, I want you to really think about becoming a coach. I know this seminar was all about coaching and motivational speaking, and I want you to really go for it, because it may be easy to go back to the old ways in Las Vegas."

His words were exactly what I needed to hear, both permission to follow this new path and gentle guidance to stay focused on what truly called me forward rather than falling back into comfortable patterns.

Sitting on the front porch of my childhood home, the same spot where I'd realized the source of my discomfort weeks earlier, I faced a practical challenge: how to finance this move and business launch. I knew I had a 401(k) from my three seasons with the Rockettes, which added up to about $12,000 sitting untouched. Taking it out would mean penalties, but it would also mean freedom to start fresh without debt or dependency.

For the first time in my life, I made a major financial decision without consulting multiple opinions. I spoke to just one friend from the conference, who offered perspective without prescription: "Gina, no one can tell you what to do. I could advise you based on financial statistics, but in this moment, you have to do what you feel is best for you."

I knew what others would say: "Don't touch retirement funds, find another way, ask for help." But something deeper was guiding me toward independence, toward trusting my own inner knowing. The decision crystallized with surprising clarity: I would cash out the 401(k), move to Las Vegas, and strategically invest in building my coaching business.

The leap of faith felt both terrifying and absolutely perfect. Each step of the process the paperwork, the bank transfers, finding a place to live carried a sense of determination and destiny. This wasn't just starting over; this was building something entirely new from everything I'd learned in recent years, from the coaching certification to the life lessons of Italy.

From March to the fall of 2013, what had begun as a tentative next step had blossomed into a full-time coaching business. My niche emerged organically: coaching dancers. I became the support I wished I'd had at twelve or thirteen, when my confidence faltered, my mental clarity needed strengthening, and my heart needed guidance. The training I'd invested in, combined with my lived experience, created a unique offering that resonated deeply with young performers and their parents.

It began with one dancer, then a referral to another, and then another parent was reaching out, until the momentum built into a sustainable practice. Each session in which I witnessed a young dancer finding their center, not just physically but emotionally and spiritually, confirmed that I was exactly where I needed to be, doing exactly what I was meant to do.

When I called my father to share my success, his first question caught me off guard: "Gina, you haven't asked us for money. How did you get this started?"

I hesitated before answering honestly: "Dad, I just couldn't tell you, but I cashed out my 401(k) in March and did what I knew I needed to do."

The silence that followed held no judgment, only respect for the woman I had become: someone who could listen to her own inner knowing, who could trust the wisdom that resides within rather than constantly seeking external validation or direction.

Starting over had led me not backward but forward into greater authenticity. The answers had been within me all along, waiting for the discomfort to grow great enough to push me into listening. Sometimes the most profound guidance comes not in moments of success but in periods of complete uncertainty, when we're stripped of familiar identities and forced to discover who we truly are beneath the makeup, the costumes, and the applause.

REVIVING THE SPIRIT

Reminders

Embrace the discomfort of not knowing: The uncertainty that feels most unbearable often precedes our greatest growth. When I sat on my parents' porch feeling like a "loser" with nothing impressive to report, I was actually being prepared for authentic reinvention.

Trust the divine bumps: What appear as random coincidences an unexpected email, a treadmill conversation, literally bumping into someone at a conference are often divine choreography orchestrating our next steps. These "coincidental" encounters carry more guidance than our most careful planning.

Listen to your inner knowing: The wisdom you seek externally often already exists within you. While advice from others has value, sometimes the most powerful decisions come from trusting your own deep knowing, even when it contradicts conventional wisdom.

STEPS

⚱ Lipstick: Remember that transformation rarely feels comfortable while it's happening. Applying lipstick or lip balm perfectly requires a steady hand through moments of uncertainty.

◉ Lashes: Pay attention to the "divine bumps" in your daily life the seemingly coincidental meetings, the unexpected opportunities, the random comments that resonate deeply. Just as eyelashes frame the windows to your soul, these encounters often frame the doorways to your future. Be willing to walk through them, even when they appear in unexpected places.

✦ God: Trust that divine wisdom often speaks in the spaces between your thoughts, in the quiet moments when you're brave enough to listen to your own heart. Start with five minutes of silence a day, gradually extending the time as you become more comfortable with this inner conversation.

PRAYER

A Prayer for Sacred Beginnings

Divine Source of Renewal,

Remind me revival comes by being more present. Help me find restoration in deeper connection.

Grant me courage to remain in the holy place of knowing that not-knowing at times, is ok. Transform uncertainty into preparation.

Open me to divine bumps and sacred nudges, those seemingly random encounters that are Your choreography. Give me ears to hear inner knowing, courage to follow despite conventional wisdom.

With ease, please, restore my weary soul through my divine inner essence.

Amen.

Part Three: The Purpose

Where surrender, unexpected connections, and divine presence reveal your authentic calling

"The most challenging dance is learning to follow rather than lead. When you release your grip on how life should unfold, step into unfamiliar temples, and allow yourself to be moved by something greater, your authentic purpose emerges with a grace your striving could never create."

THE ISLAND OF REMEMBERING

"In stepping away from everything familiar, you may discover what truly matters has been within you all along." GP

When God Removes You to Restore You
Age 31-32 | New York City to Sardinia, Italy

Divine timing has a way of appearing in the spaces between our plans. There I was, living in New York City after three seasons as a Radio City Rockette, waiting to hear if I'd be hired for a fourth season. My professional dance life had become a series of auditions, performances, and constant hustle, the rhythm of the city matching my own internal tempo of always moving forward, always pushing harder, and always reaching for the next achievement.

A part of me felt exhausted, questioning who I was and what my purpose might be. Something deep inside whispered that a change was coming, yet the autopilot part of me kept pushing toward the familiar, the comfortable, the known path. I loved my one-bedroom apartment in Sunnyside, Queens. I loved my windowsill where I could sit and think. I loved knowing I was dancing in the Big Apple and paying my own rent. But as other dancers received their calls about rejoining the kickline, and my phone remained silent, that beloved windowsill became my therapist.

Three days passed without a shower, my emotions sinking lower, my spirit falling into a funk. I hadn't spoken to anyone during this time until my father's name appeared on my cell phone screen. Somehow, he always knew when to call. The divine often speaks through the people who love us most deeply.

"Gina, what's going on?" His voice carried equal measures of worry and intuition.

"Dad, I feel down," I admitted, hearing the defeat in my own words. "I don't think I made it again, and I'm stuck." The poor-me tone in my voice surprised even me, evidence of a surrender so unlike my usual determination.

My father's response arrived like a lifeline thrown to someone drowning: "Gina, you need to remember the Gina Pero I know. The little girl who shoveled snow just to practice her solo, the girl who wore a back brace for five years and still danced, the girl who goes after her dreams no matter what, the girl who tells me God has a plan."

Tears rolled down my face as I fell to my knees near the windowsill. My father's words became my strength, his voice an anchor, his message the fuel I needed to rise again. Sometimes the divine speaks most clearly through those we trust, who can remind us of who we are even when we've temporarily forgotten.

His call gave me just enough energy to shower and attend my friend's reconnective healing yoga class. During the session, as my friend guided my body toward alignment, the healing continued. She spoke about purpose and trusting one's path, everything I needed to hear to keep taking one step at a time. I left feeling centered, alive, and ready to handle whatever outcome awaited my one precious life.

Walking out of yoga, my phone lit up with an unexpected call. "Hey Gina, I'm in New York again from Italy and I was wondering if you could meet me for lunch?" It was Miss Lori, the ballet teacher who had taught me when I was twelve. Her voice instantly transported me back to earlier days of barre exercises and patient corrections. There was always something magical about Miss Lori's spirit, something that transcended her role as a dance instructor.

I hadn't seen her in three years, not since our chance encounter in Manhattan when she had first extended an invitation I had promptly declined: "Would you consider moving to Sardinia, Italy to teach at my dance studio?"

"No, no," I had responded without hesitation back then. "I just got to New York. I'm living my dance dreams." Dreams that included performing on prestigious stages, establishing myself in the dance capital of the world. Dreams I had been chasing since those early days at David DeMarie Dance Studio, when I first discovered the indent on the right side of my body that would shape so much of my professional dance journey.

Now, three years later, sitting across from Miss Lori and her daughter at lunch, the same invitation floated between us once more: "You know, the offer is still on the table. If you would like to move to Sardinia and teach for me, and be a part of our dance studio, I would love to have you anytime."

Something shifted inside me as she spoke, a sensation both unfamiliar and deeply recognizable, like discovering a room in your childhood home you somehow never noticed before. A quiet "yes" began to resonate within me, not from my mind with its carefully constructed plans, but from somewhere deeper, a place that recognized truth before reason could analyze it. As I pondered if this was the change I had been sensing, a favorite quote played inside my mind: "What's for you will never pass you by."

Walking out of the restaurant after lunch, the universe arranged another piece of the divine puzzle. There on the sidewalk stood my friend, a fellow Rockette. I asked, "Do you know if they are done hiring for next season?" Her casual response landed with the weight of confirmation: "Yeah, the season's full." In that moment, I knew with absolute certainty that this wasn't just bad news about a job; it was divine redirection. The universe was ensuring I understood that one door had closed so I could walk through another one that led across an ocean. As Miss Lori wanted an answer right away, I decided to call Radio City myself for one more divine confirmation.

The news was as I'd expected: *Ladies and gentlemen, Gina Pero will not be eye-high kicking for Christmas.*

As soon as I received this divine notification, I called Miss Lori to create a plan. Those four days with Lynn only weeks before this divine appointment had prepared me, and now six weeks later, I boarded a plane with a one-way ticket to Sardinia, my heart both lighter and more expanded than it had been in years. The hustle of New York, the auditions, the competition, the constant strive to prove and improve fell away with each mile that carried me over the Atlantic. My body, which had endured back braces, ankle injuries, and a concussion that had literally knocked me into a new direction, now relaxed into the possibility of something different.

"Bring a bathing suit and change of clothes in your carry-on," Miss Lori instructed, "because I'm taking you to the beach as soon as you land." When the plane touched down on the Mediterranean island, I stepped into a world that operated according to entirely different rules than the ones I'd left behind. Instead of rushing me to my new apartment or diving into teaching schedules, Miss Lori drove me directly to a beach with water so crystal blue it seemed almost unreal, like stepping into a postcard rather than an actual place.

She had packed a small panini for me, a simple act of nurturing care very different from the grab-and-go mentality I'd grown accustomed to in New York. Standing there with my toes in the warm sand, arms stretched wide to embrace this new beginning, I felt something bubble up from deep within: pure, unfiltered joy. A friend later saw a photo of me taken in that moment and remarked, "Gina, I've never seen you this happy."

That observation prompted me to reflect on why God might have brought me to this island, so far from the familiar rhythms of my professional dance career. Initially, I thought it was about giving back through teaching, about enjoying pasta and wine, about experiencing a different culture. But as days turned into weeks, I began to understand there was something much deeper unfolding, a divine curriculum designed specifically for what my spirit needed to remember.

The people of Sardinia became my unwitting teachers, their daily routines a masterclass in what I had forgotten about living well. Every morning, warm greetings of "*Ciao Bella, Buon giorno!*" flowed from neighbors, shopkeepers, and students. Their voices carried a musical quality that seemed to vibrate at a higher frequency than the rushed exchanges I was used to. The fragrance of flowers growing wild around my neighborhood offered sensory invitations to pause and breathe deeply, to actually notice and appreciate what was already present rather than racing toward what was next.

Perhaps most striking was the sacred ritual of lunch. Each day around one o'clock, the streets would fall eerily silent, as if someone had pressed a cosmic pause button on the entire community. You could drop a pin and hear it fall, as the saying goes. This wasn't just a meal; it was a sacrament of sorts. Families gathered together, food prepared with intention, conversation and connection prioritized over productivity. No phones, no multitasking, no quick bites between appointments. Just presence with food and loved ones.

Evenings carried their own gentle ritual. Around five o'clock, my computer would suddenly feel out of place as Miss Lori or another friend would gently but firmly suggest, "Gina, you need to put that thing away. It's time to rest and just be together." Gathering around a small fire, sharing cheese and wine, and engaging in unhurried conversations gave me a glimpse of what life could feel like.

This new rhythm didn't come easily to someone who had spent years perfecting the art of maximizing every moment. "*Calma*, Gina," they would tell me when my New York energy would surge forward. "Relax, *tranquilla*." Sometimes they would place their hands on my shoulders, as if physically lowering the altitude of my anxiety. "*Pazienza*, my dear Gina," they would say, smiling at my American urgency to accomplish, complete, advance.

These weren't just cultural differences; they were divine interventions. As these gentle corrections continued, I began to see the truth: God hadn't brought me to Sardinia just to teach dance but to be taught how to truly live. I had become so wrapped up in work, in doing, in achieving, that I had forgotten the sacred art of being. The island, with its different rhythms and values, was a divine recovery room where I could remember what my soul had known before the professional dance world trained it otherwise.

The island removed me from all the noise, both external and internal, that had been drowning out the voice of my authentic self. Teaching dance in a language I barely spoke forced me to communicate differently, to rely more on presence than performance. Having only one or two English-speaking friends challenged me to find connection beyond words. Being away from everything familiar required me to discover what remained when all the external markers of identity were stripped away. In that stripping away, I found something unexpected: a deeper sense of presence than I had ever known before.

Through sunset rituals, shared meals, and neighborhood connections, I learned home inside myself wasn't about being in a specific location it was a way of being. I learned that taking time for myself, relaxing without agenda, sharing unhurried moments with friends, and eating whole foods with appreciation were daily rituals training me. I learned that setting aside technology to be in the moment and celebrating natural beauty as a daily practice, rather than an occasional indulgence, was a coming home to myself.

Living on the third floor of a local family's apartment building, I experienced perhaps the most profound lesson of all. One day, Mama Loredana from downstairs knocked on my door, a home-cooked lunch in hand. It was a simple gesture, but it struck something so deep within me that tears immediately sprang to my eyes.

"Thank you," I managed to say, overwhelmed by the unexpected offering.

In that moment of receiving, I recognized a block I hadn't even known existed. When was the last time I had allowed someone to nurture me so simply, without feeling I needed to earn it or reciprocate immediately? When had I last offered such uncomplicated care to someone else, without an agenda or expectation? This wasn't just about food, although I call myself a foodie; it was about the fundamental human exchange of giving and receiving care. This exchange became distorted when I chose to prioritize independence and achievement above interdependence and presence.

Invitations to join the family for breakfast, lunch, and dinner became regular occurrences. They weren't just feeding me meals; they were nourishing my starving spirit with the kind of community I had been too busy to cultivate. They were showing me, through simple daily acts, what it meant to truly live in relationship rather than in isolation.

The small third-level apartment became a sanctuary of rediscovery. Each night, I would sneak out and climb out the window onto an unfurnished rooftop, hoping I wouldn't wake up the family below me. As the sky became dark, all I could see was the illuminated cross that stood as a beacon over the city of Olbia. I knew I was not alone. This vision reconnected me to one of my spiritual practices that I had set aside in the busyness of professional dance, The Rosary. I learned The Rosary as a young child in Catholic grade school and came to love it sitting on my Nana's couch, sharing this practice with her.

In those late hours on the rooftop, I would dance freely until two or three in the morning, practicing not the choreographed precision of a Rockette but the spontaneous expression of a soul remembering its voice. This wasn't a performance, but a prayer. The Rosary became my song. The movement, my prayer. It was a dance that emerged from authentic connection rather than external expectation.

When the family downstairs eventually mentioned hearing me dancing in the middle of the night, I realized that what had begun as private devotion had become a testament that others could sense. Mama Lori Donna intuitively handed me a rosary as a gift, and in that exchange, divine confirmation hit me like a lightning bolt in the most loving way. I knew I was exactly where I was supposed to be, and with the people I was supposed to be with.

Before going to Sardinia, a part of me had wanted to quit dance. My body had messaged me signs of exhaustion and overwhelm, and my passion was burnt out. As I began to slowly find my rhythm again, dancing on the rooftop, I knew that if anyone would be able to help bring my dance passion to life again, it would be Miss Lori. Watching Miss Lori as a young girl was like watching a spirit soar. Her flawless technique and generous love for the art inspired me to move. As I approached Miss Lori with this awareness, she invited me to perform solo in the upcoming dance recital. She wanted me to share my gifts with the dancers I had been teaching all year long. Although I knew I would have to stretch myself to perform again, I also knew that beyond the stretch was an invitation to remember that dance was an art to be shared.

Choosing a jazz solo to dance to the sound of one of my cousin's recorded trumpet tracks, spiraling through the studio like golden threads of light, reconnected me to the essence of dance, not as achievement but as an offering. Each movement flowed, not from my formal training but from something deeper, more honest. As the stage lights warmed my skin, and I gazed into the eyes of my students, a profound recognition washed over me: This is who Gina Pero truly is. Not a performer desperate for validation or a technician executing steps with precision, but an artist expressing her unique voice through movement. In that sacred moment of connection, I understood that my worth wasn't tied to which kickline I joined or which stage I conquered, but to the authentic expression that only my body, with its particular history and wisdom, could offer the world. Our deepest purpose isn't found in accomplishing or acquiring but in remembering and embodying the truth of who we've always been.

This is exactly what this book is about, reviving our spirits with practices that actually nourish rather than deplete us. In the hustle to become a Rockette again and again and again, I had forgotten the very things that had originally drawn me to dance: joy, expression, connection, presence. I had traded the essence for the achievement, the being for the doing.

Sardinia restored these forgotten essentials through daily invitations to slow down and savor: extraordinary food prepared with care and enjoyed without rush; genuine connection with people who prioritized relationship over productivity; the sensory delight of fragrant flowers, crystal waters, and painterly sunsets; the rhythm of days shaped by natural beauty rather than artificial deadlines.

My favorite words coming back to the states were, "*Grazie mille,*" translating to "a thousand thanks."

These essential nutrients were exactly what my spirit had been silently starving for. In removing me from everything familiar, God had invited me to this magical island to help me remember who I was, and what truly mattered most. To the people, places, and things in Sardinia, grazie mille!

REVIVING THE SPIRIT

Reminders

Divine redirection often requires removal: The very distance that seems like disconnection becomes the space where deeper connection can emerge. When a door closes, like my fourth Rockette season, it's often divine protection creating room for something more aligned with our authentic purpose.

The spiritual practice of receiving: Allowing others to care for us without immediate reciprocation can be more challenging than giving. Learning to graciously receive, whether it's a home-cooked meal or a community's embrace, is not passive but a profound spiritual practice.

Presence is the ultimate prayer: The rituals of Sardinian life shared meals, sunset viewings, unhurried conversations taught me that being fully present is itself a form of devotion. When we slow down enough to actually taste our food, listen without formulating our next response, and appreciate beauty without capturing it for social media, we enter sacred time where the divine can reach us more directly.

STEPS

🬀 Lipstick: Express, "I know I am capable of presence and productivity." Notice the sensations that arise in your body as you speak these words. Notice how this small action of a simple sentence begins to shift your relationship with yourself.

👁 Lashes: Look for the "lunch-bringers" in your life, those who offer simple care without an agenda. See how acknowledging their gift deepens your capacity to receive.

✦ God: The divine often speaks through beauty we're too rushed to notice. Stand by a window, step outside, or even look at online sunset images. Allow this moment of natural wonder to reconnect you to something larger than your daily concerns.

PRAYER

Finding Home Within Yourself

God of Inner Dwelling,

Help me remember that a true home is not a physical location but spiritual recognition. When circumstances shift, anchor me in the unchanging truth within.

Remind me that wherever I go, whatever stages I perform, I carry within the sacred temple of Your presence. Grant grace to return to this inner sanctuary when outer storms rage.

Slow my hurried pace, quiet rushing thoughts. In shared meals, sunset moments, unhurried conversations, help me enter divine time where You speak clearly.

With ease, please, strip away layers of doing to help me remember the art of being.

Amen.

SACRED FIRE

"The sacred isn't confined to designated holy places but exists wherever you approach with an open heart. Your prayers can travel across oceans. Your connection to the divine is available everywhere, even in the most ordinary moments of your day." GP

Finding God in Unexpected Temples
Age 24 | Tokyo, Japan

Incense and cherry blossoms. The first breath of Tokyo filled my lungs with scents both foreign and intoxicating as I stepped from the climate-controlled airport into the humid embrace of Japan. My body, accustomed to the precise measurements of American dance studios, now stood disoriented yet thrilled on soil that had never felt the pressure of my particular footsteps. The soft weight of my passport pressed against my chest in its travel pouch was a tangible reminder that I was actually here, about to perform as one of two dancers in a magician show at the Shinagawa Prince Hotel.

My fingers instinctively traced the subtle curve in my spine, that familiar terrain of scoliosis that had once threatened to end my dance career before it began. How many doctors had examined that same curve with furrowed brows? How many had suggested that perhaps dance wasn't the wisest choice for a body like mine? Yet here I stood, oceans away from those limiting prognoses, my imperfect form about to create beauty on an international stage. The universe has a magnificent way of transforming our supposed limitations into unexpected passageways to adventure. The flight had been its own suspended reality, a twenty-hour choreography of service carts, dim lighting, and the gentle hum of engines that vibrated through the soles of my feet. I'd watched the flight map on my screen, the tiny animated plane inching its way across a digital ocean, and marveled at how dance had literally moved me across the world. Through the window, clouds stretched like an endless white stage beneath us, occasionally parting to reveal glimpses of the shimmering Pacific, a blue so deep it seemed to hold the sky's reflection in perfect balance.

Tokyo immediately enveloped me in a symphony that awakened every sense. Neon signs cast their electric glow across rain-slicked streets, creating a dance of color and reflection that made even puddles seem intentional. The melodic rise and fall of Japanese announcements flowed through train stations like a choreographed sound, a language I couldn't translate but somehow felt in my body. The subtle symphony of unfamiliar spices ginger, sesame, miso drifted from restaurant doorways, intertwining with the clean scent of efficiency that seemed to characterize everything in this meticulously organized city. Tokyo moved with its own unique rhythm, performing a dance I was eager to learn.

After landing, we rehearsed for hours, our jet-lagged bodies summoning muscle memory when conscious direction failed. Sweat traced familiar pathways along my hairline, rolling down my temples as I moved through sequences that my mind was too tired to direct. The studio floors felt different beneath my bare feet, smoother somehow, with a particular give that spoke of quality and care. Even through exhaustion, I registered how the Japanese attention to detail extended to the very surface beneath my movements. My body, ever my most honest teacher, was making new connections with this foreign space.

"Five, six, seven, eight," our choreographer counted, and despite the eighteen-hour time difference, my limbs responded with the precision built through years of training. My muscles remembered what my disoriented mind could not seem to grasp. Isn't that the way of wisdom? Often our bodies understand truths that our conscious thoughts haven't yet processed.

Taking a deep breath as I walked into my hotel room for the first time, I was struck by the elegant simplicity of the space: clean lines, minimal decoration, and absolute functionality. The sheets on the bed held the particular crispness of high-quality cotton, the air carried the subtle scent of something floral but not overpowering. But it was the bathroom that truly captured my attention, specifically the toilet. This wasn't just any toilet. It had heated seats that welcomed my tired body with unexpected warmth and a control panel with more buttons than my first cell phone. It had a gadget with settings for water temperature and pressure. It was the Ferrari of toilets.

I called my dad immediately from the hotel phone, unable to contain my excitement about this unexpected discovery. My father, a plumber by trade, would appreciate the technical details in a way few others would. The phone connection crackled slightly, adding distance to his familiar voice when he answered.

"Dad," I exclaimed, barely giving him time to say hello, "this is the exact toilet seat that I want when I have my own house one day." My voice echoed with childlike excitement in the pristine bathroom. We laughed together across the miles and time zones, connected by this oddly intimate conversation. After all, who likes to sit on a cool toilet seat? The Japanese had it figured out: Warm your tush, and it will be a lot easier to, well, you know what.

Walking into the theater that day, tush ready, I was taken by surprise. Instead of the massive venue I'd envisioned, it was an intimate dinner theater where the audience sat close enough to see every expression, every intentional detail of our costumes. Stage lights cast pools of gold and amber across the floor during our tech rehearsal, transforming simple movements into illusions as shadows danced alongside us. The space held a magical quality, with acoustics that carried music directly to the heart and sightlines that created connection between performer and witness. I loved it immediately, this perfect container for what we were about to create: magic itself.

On opening night, excitement vibrated through the backstage area as word spread that Japanese dignitaries would be attending. The air felt charged with a different kind of energy, part nervousness, part reverence. The significance wasn't lost on me; this wasn't just any audience member but a figure of historical and cultural importance. As I applied my stage makeup, fingers slightly trembling with the weight of the moment, I could hear the audience gathering, their hushed conversations creating a gentle hum beyond the curtain.

The performance itself became a blur of muscle and music, light and illusion. My body moved with a freedom that surprised me, as if the distance from home had somehow released me from certain limitations I'd carried. There's something about performing in a foreign country that strips away familiar insecurities. No one here knew my history, my struggles, my doubts. They saw only what I presented in this moment, and somehow that awareness lifted me into a different quality of movement.

Afterward, I remember eating the most delicious fruit I had ever tasted succulent, perfectly ripened, and arranged with artistic precision that made each piece look like an edible jewel. The sweetness burst across my tongue, juice threatening to run down my chin as I savored each bite. It was transcendent, another reminder that I had traveled far from the familiar supermarket produce of home. The chef had presented each fruit in its perfect moment of ripeness, teaching me through this simple offering that timing is everything in cooking, in dance, in life itself.

The audience's reception warmed my performer's heart. Their applause carried a particular rhythm and excitement, most bowed their heads to say hello and thank you, a gesture that engaged their entire body in respect. The applause felt genuine. The audience was eager to meet us. Their eyes bright with appreciation, they expressed gratitude for our performance. I felt like a star, or what I imagined a star might feel like, valued not just for what I did but for bringing beauty and art into their evening.

On day five of my trip, reality intruded on this magical experience. I called my dad for our daily check-in, settling onto the edge of my hotel bed, the phone pressed to my ear. The connection was clear that day, which made the hesitation in his voice all the more apparent. I could hear immediately that something was different in his tone, which was weighed down by a heaviness that traveled across oceans and continents to reach me. He didn't want to share difficult news with me while I was so far away, but I could tell from the way he cleared his throat multiple times that something was wrong. Eventually, the words came: my Nana, another wise grandmother in my life, my spiritual mentor, a woman I spoke to every other day, his mom, had been diagnosed with cancer.

My jaw dropped as I sat on the edge of the bed, phone pressed to my ear so tightly it hurt, trying to process what he was saying. The hotel room suddenly felt alien, the perfect corners and minimal design now cold rather than elegant. The distance from home felt insurmountable, causing a physical ache that spread across my chest. How was I supposed to help from the other side of the world? What was I supposed to do? Fly home immediately? Stay and fulfill my professional commitment? All these questions surfaced in my mind, creating a storm of uncertainty that made it hard to breathe.

I was sad. I was scared. My grandma was one of my best friends, a cornerstone of my life. She was the woman who had taught me The Rosary and was a living example of faith. She had also taught me adages like "the lord helps those who help themselves," "mind your ps and qs," and "watch out for wandering hand trouble," which she called WHT. At times, she was the only person who saw and understood me the only one I knew I could call to feel like I was enough. Now she was facing her own battle, and I was separated by oceans and continents, my body unable to be where my heart already was, by her side. So I did what I knew I could do: I picked up the hotel phone and called her.

"Nana," I said trying to hold back my tears, "It's Gina calling you from Japan."

"Gina! I hope you're not paying for this call." Her first words made me laugh, as I realized I actually didn't know what the call was costing me.

"Gina," she shared, "I know you may be worried about me, but I want you to pray for me ..." My Nana, being a prayer warrior and teaching me the power of prayer my entire life, was now asking me to pray for her. Something she had never asked of me before. Of course I told her I would do just that, and we hung up quickly. The next day, seeking comfort in the familiar rituals of my faith, I approached our hotel manager and asked if she could tell me where the closest Catholic church was. She looked at me with genuine curiosity, her head tilting slightly as she considered my request. "A Catholic church in Japan?" she repeated, as if making sure she'd heard correctly. "Let me see what I can do." Her response wasn't dismissive, but it made me realize I was asking for something that might not be readily available.

In the meantime, I went to the cafe downstairs, a place that had already become a comfortable haven during my stay. The aroma of freshly ground coffee mingled with the subtle sweetness of traditional Japanese confections as I pulled up my email to see if there was anything important. The cafe at our hotel was quiet enough for reflection but lively enough to feel connected to the pulse of Tokyo.

Sipping my tea, the warmth spreading through my hands from the perfectly sized ceramic cup, I started asking a newfound friend who worked at the cafe if she knew where a Catholic church was. After several confused looks and apologetic headshakes, my friend took my hand and offered me an alternative suggestion. She said, "Gina, here in Japan, we have temples that provide a space for reflection and prayer. I know you will find peace there." I admitted that I didn't know what a temple was. The response came from a place of genuine curiosity rather than resistance. Something in her suggestion resonated with a deeper part of me, the part that had always sensed God's presence beyond the confines of formal structures. The same part that had felt divine presence in dance studios, on stages, and in the quiet moments of connection with my own imperfect body.

The very next day, following my friend's detailed directions, I walked to the temple. The morning air carried a cool crispness that awakened my senses, the sidewalks already bustling with purposeful movement. From a distance, the temple looked like a park, serene greenery surrounding traditional Japanese architecture. As I approached the entrance, nervousness fluttered in my stomach like butterflies before a performance. I felt like I was supposed to follow protocols I didn't understand and honor traditions I had never been taught. My body was unsure of which positions to assume in this unfamiliar sacred space.

Taking a deep breath, the scent of incense already reaching me from within, I stepped through the gate. Immediately, I noticed a beautiful fire burning in a large ceremonial cauldron. Orange and yellow flames danced upward, creating a living column of light that seemed to connect earth and sky. The fire crackled softly, each pop and hiss creating a natural percussion that invited presence. The heat from it reached out to touch my face even from several feet away, a gentle reminder of its power and purpose. I didn't know what to call this sacred vessel, not an altar exactly, but clearly a focal point for prayer and intention.

Through careful observation, I discovered that when you walked in, you first set your intention or your prayer and put it in the fire, whether written on paper or simply held in your heart. Then you could find a quiet place to sit. I watched others before me, observing their reverence, the way they approached the fire with intention. Their movements held the grace of long practice, bodies enacting faith through familiar gestures.

As a dancer, I recognized the choreography of worship immediately, the way these strangers moved with intention toward the fire, the precise gestures they made, the rhythm of their approach and retreat. Faith, I realized, is often expressed through the body's wisdom before the mind's understanding. In that moment, I understood that while the specific movements differed from the genuflections and signs of the cross that I'd grown up with, the essential choreography of reverence was strikingly similar.

Following the example of others, I approached the fire, its warmth intensifying with each step. In my heart, I held my Nana, visualizing her wrapped in healing light, trying to send love across the impossible distance between us. I thought of my father, carrying the weight of his mother's illness while trying to protect me from worry. I thought of my own journey, how far I had come from the girl with the back brace and the doubting heart. Then I released these thoughts into the flames, watching as they seemed to rise higher for just a moment, as if acknowledging my offering, the fire dancing with new energy as my prayers joined countless others.

Finding a quiet bench beneath a cherry tree, not yet in bloom but holding the promise of future blossoms, I sat in meditation. The wood of the bench felt smooth beneath my fingertips, worn by countless others who had sat here before me seeking connection, answers, comfort. Around me, the sounds of the temple created their own gentle music: the occasional ring of a bell that sent vibrations through the air, the soft footsteps of visitors on gravel paths, the distant murmur of prayers or conversations. A breeze stirred the branches above me, whispering secrets in a language I couldn't translate but somehow understood. Here, thousands of miles from the churches of my upbringing, I found something unexpected, a sense of sacred presence that transcended cultural boundaries.

I realized at that moment that God wasn't confined to Catholic churches or any particular religious structure. The divine was here in this temple, in the sacred fire that transformed prayers into light, in the peaceful countenance of those who came to worship in their way. It was in the cherry tree above me, dormant now but preparing for glorious renewal. It was in my own body, still capable of creating beauty through movement despite its imperfections. It was in the air I breathed, shared with strangers whose language I couldn't speak but whose humanity I recognized instantly. It was in nature all around me. God was everywhere.

What a revelation, that prayer could travel across oceans more effectively than any phone call, that spiritual connection required no particular building or ritual, that the divine presence I'd always sought in specific places had been available to me everywhere, always. I thought of the countless hours I'd spent in dance studios, feeling something transcendent in the connection between music and movement. Had that been prayer too? Had God been present in every plié, every turn, every moment when my imperfect body achieved something beautiful?

For the remainder of my time in Japan, I returned to the temple daily. Sometimes I would simply sit, allowing the peace of the place to wash over me like gentle rain, cleansing my worry and fear about my Nana. In the midst of my concern for her, I found a center of calm, a way to connect with something larger than my fear. My body, so far from home, found a new kind of belonging in this ancient space. It also felt a new way of prayer, of spiritual connection. I began to learn that even though we may be far away from loved ones, prayer travels, and your energy of love can be felt millions of miles away.

I called my Nana every day from the hotel phone on that trip. The phone bill was not my priority. At that time, things like WhatsApp and checking emails on a cell phone didn't exist. I either had to use the hotel room phone or go down to a pay phone to make a call. To check emails, I went to the cafe and used a computer there. Technology was not attached to my waist or pulling me into distraction. The journey of presence, of prayer, and time on my hotel phone was well spent.

On this particular trip, I received an email from a very close high school friend asking for help. He mentioned he had tried calling me only to find out I was in Tokyo. "You have become so prestigious, so professional, I hope your dreams are becoming a reality," he said. "I guess I'm asking for a pep talk from you, for some motivation," he continued, "Gina, I'm very proud of you, I wish you the best, please help me to become the best that I can become." This message came so suddenly, I immediately went to the pay phone to call him, concerned. I wonder, what if I hadn't?

Years later, during my third season with the Rockettes, I got a phone call about that same friend, informing me that he had passed away far too young. I remember sitting in my dressing room that day, phone in hand, hearing the news. What I heard over the phone that day I will never forget, "Gina, you may never know the impact you had, how your words of encouragement were words that got him through during many days." You see, we may never know the impact of a phone call, or time spent encouraging someone, or even words and messages that impact someone's life. The question is, are you willing to make the call, no matter what the cost?

The journey to Tokyo opened up so many things for me, thanks in part to its distance from everything I knew. It gave me more than professional experience and cultural exposure. It expanded my understanding of the divine, teaching me that sacred spaces exist everywhere, in Japanese temples with their ceremonial fires, in hospital rooms where loved ones fight for health, and in our own imperfect bodies as they move through the world creating beauty. The God I had always known was bigger than I had imagined, and finding Him in unexpected temples and inside myself had been the greatest gift of my journey. My body, with all its history and wisdom, had once again led me to exactly where I needed to be, proving that sometimes we must travel far from home to discover what we already carry within us.

When I returned to the United States, I discovered the full extent of my international calls. The cost of my phone bill in those five weeks was the same as my incoming check for performing. Every dollar I had earned dancing in that magical theater had been spent connecting with the people I loved across impossible distances. There was the daily call to Nana, the lengthy conversation with my troubled friend, the check-ins with my worried father. Not a penny remained for savings.

Some might call this poor financial planning. According to conventional wisdom, it was. But as I held that phone bill in my hands, the pages upon pages detailing each expensive connection, a different kind of accounting came to mind. What was the value of speaking to my grandmother during what I thought would be her final months? What price could I put on the words that carried my friend through dark days? What was the worth of hearing my father's voice as we navigated difficulty together, despite the oceans between us?

These connections, these bridges built of words and silence, of prayer and presence, had been my true work in Japan, as essential as any dance I performed on stage. The numbers on that bill weren't just costs; they were investments in what mattered most. They were evidence of love made tangible, of priorities aligned with purpose.

I folded the bill and tucked it away, not with regret but with a strange sense of peace. I had spent everything I earned on what could not be measured, on what would last far longer than any souvenir or saved dollar. The question that haunts me still, that I offer to you now, is simply this: If I hadn't chosen to spend money on those phone calls that one summer afar, what would it really have cost me?

There are moments in life when the most practical choice is the one that makes no practical sense at all. When the wisest investment yields no financial return but pays dividends in connection, in meaning, in the quiet certainty that when it mattered most, you reached across the distance. You made the call. You chose love over ledgers. And in doing so, you discovered what was sacred all along.

REVIVING THE SPIRIT

Reminders

Sacred spaces transcend boundaries: What we recognize as "holy" often depends on what we've been taught to see. When we open ourselves to finding the divine in unfamiliar settings, whether a Japanese temple, a hospital room, or our own imperfect bodies, we discover that God speaks in many languages and dwells in countless forms.

Distance creates new perspectives: Sometimes being physically removed from our familiar environment, even when that removal feels painful or disruptive, allows us to see our lives and faith from a new angle. Trust that even geographical separation from loved ones during difficult times can serve a greater purpose in your and their spiritual growth.

Ritual transcends religion: The human desire to set intentions, make offerings, and find physical expressions for spiritual connection is universal. Whether lighting candles in a Catholic church, or simply sitting in quiet meditation, these rituals connect us to something larger than ourselves.

STEPS

⚱ Lipstick: Make a sacred connection call this week. Just as I called my Nana and a friend from Tokyo despite the cost, identify someone in your life who needs to hear your voice, not just a text or email. Notice how crossing the distance with your voice becomes its own kind of sacred offering, a prayer made tangible through technology.

◉ Lashes: Look beyond the familiar structures you associate with spirituality. Visit a place of worship from a tradition different from your own, whether a temple, mosque, synagogue, or indigenous sacred site. Enter with respect, appreciation, and openness.

✦ God: When facing a challenge that seems impossible to solve within your current framework, whether a health crisis, a relationship difficulty, or a creative block, ask yourself: "Where might God be speaking to me in unexpected ways about this situation?" Pay attention to coincidences, to suggestions that initially seem unrelated to your faith tradition, to solutions that come from unlikely sources. Remember that divine wisdom often arrives through channels we wouldn't think to look for it.

PRAYER

Divine Guidance in Unexpected Places

Divine Presence in All Places,

Open my eyes to Your guidance in unexpected places and unlikely messengers. Help me recognize You in unfamiliar temples, new rituals, foreign languages, silent spaces between heartbeats.

When seeking answers, remind me You speak through many forms. Grant wisdom to make impractical choices when love demands them, to reach across distances when someone needs my voice.

Help me remember prayer travels faster than technology, connection transcends geography, my presence requires no passport. Nothing truly separates us. Remind me that the most sacred investment is never measured in dollars.

With ease, please, attune my spirit to hear Your voice however and wherever it speaks.

Amen

DIVINE SURRENDER

"True surrender isn't weakness but a different kind of strength the courage to trust while remaining fully yourself. In releasing your grip on how you think things should unfold, you create space for how they're actually meant to unfold." Gina Pero

When Following Becomes Freedom
Age 33-36 | Las Vegas

Las Vegas welcomed me back like an old friend with new stories to tell. The city where I'd first performed professionally, where I'd dreamed of stages and spotlights, now became the stage for an entirely different performance. The divine knockout that had ended my Rockettes career had actually been positioning me for this, though I didn't yet know that my greatest performance would be learning to trust, to follow, to love.

The neon lights of Las Vegas pulsed against the indigo desert sky as I drove down the Strip, windows down, letting the warm air tangle my hair. Four years had passed since my divine knockout at Radio City , since

God had literally knocked me off the stage to redirect my path. Now I was back in the city where my professional dance journey had begun, but everything about me had changed.

I never imagined returning to Vegas. After becoming a Rockette, after the concussion that ended that dream, after discovering my true calling as a coach, why would God bring me back to this desert city of manufactured dreams?

The answer had come in divinely orchestrated stages. First, through Sardinia's gift of stripping away everything non-essential. Then through the discomfort of living in my parents' attic, where being without impressive titles forced me to find worth beyond achievement. The coaching conference in Los Angeles. The "divine bump" with the speaker who needed an opening dance number. Suddenly, Vegas wasn't my past it was my future, calling me back not to reclaim old dreams but to birth new ones.

Setting up my coaching practice here felt like coming full circle. The same studios where I'd once pushed my body to its limits became healing spaces where I taught others to honor their bodies' wisdom. The city that had once represented external achievement transformed into a laboratory for internal growth.

Then came the unexpected invitation that would change everything.

"Gina, a friend is looking for a dancer and co-choreographer for a show with Meatloaf. Would you be interested?" My ballet teacher's words hung in the air like a divine whisper.

Dance as performance? After all I'd been through? My body tensed at the thought. But something deeper whispered, Pay attention. This matters.

"Just show up as you are today," she said, reading my hesitation. "That's all anyone can do."

The audition became a revelation. Meatloaf himself called me over mid-combination. "The reason I stopped you," he said with unexpected gentleness, "is because you don't need to look at anyone else to know what you're doing. You're not dancing to impress anyone. You're dancing from something real inside."

He saw in me what my journey had cultivated: presence over perfection, authenticity over technique. The show immediately became sacred space where my rebuilt relationship with dance could flourish. Each night, as Meatloaf improvised and shifted the performance, I discovered joy in adapting, in being fully present, in trusting the moment.

But even as my professional life expanded launching my podcast, developing my clothing line a deeper question surfaced during quiet moments. Sitting on my patio watching desert stars emerge, I wondered: Is there someone I'm meant to share this journey with?

The vulnerability of that question surprised me. After past wounds, I'd built walls around my heart. But something was shifting. I transformed the question into prayer: "God, show me how I can create me into the woman that my life partner can find and deeply love. "

This sacred surrender opened unexpected doors. When social dance entered my life, it terrified me. Learning to follow felt like standing at the edge of a cliff after a lifetime of solid ground. As a professional dancer accustomed to controlling every movement, the idea of letting someone else lead challenged everything I knew.

During one of my early social dance night outs, fumbling through basic steps and fighting every lead, I noticed a dancer whose movement quality stood apart from everyone else. His name was Angel, and there was something about the way he danced patiently, clear, respectful that made me want to understand this new language of partnership. "Would you like to dance?" I asked him one evening.

From our very first dance together, Angel's lead felt different. He guided without demanding, suggested without controlling.

That one-night dance experience, led us to begin our divine dancing partnership. Night after night hired at the MGM Park, under the stars that would later witness my life's most pivotal moment, Angel helped me understand that following wasn't weakness but a different kind of strength. The dance floor became my classroom for life's deeper lessons.

"You're fighting the lead," he said gently during one practice. "Trust that I won't let you fall."

His words pierced straight to my core fear the same fear that had kept me clutching my father's hand outside kindergarten, the same fear that made wearing a back brace feel like wearing my vulnerability on the outside. But with each dance, each performance, something was melting. The ice around my heart was becoming water, flowing instead of frozen.

We began performing regularly at the MGM Park. Under the open desert sky, with music flowing through the night air, I was learning the sacred art of trust not just in dance but in life. Each performance built my confidence, each successful follow expanded my capacity for surrender.

Then came the divine appointment I hadn't seen coming.

A mutual friend approached me with knowing certainty. "Gina, I really think you should meet someone. His name is Dr. Stella. You two should go for coffee."

The conviction in her voice reminded me of other pivotal moments, my dance teacher selecting my solo song, Lynn Simonson inviting me to Seattle, Miss Lisa saying "I believe in you." I'd learned to pay attention when people spoke with that particular quality of knowing.

"Okay," I agreed, trusting the divine nudge.

That first coffee felt surprisingly natural. Dr. Stella and I talked easily, discovering shared values and complementary energies. But when we hugged goodbye, something extraordinary happened. A profound calm washed through my entire body not just emotional peace but a physical sensation, as if every cell suddenly exhaled years of held tension.

I sat in my car afterward, trying to process what had just occurred. My aunt's prophetic words from years ago whispered through my memory: "You'll know by the way he touches you."

A few more meetings followed, each revealing deeper layers of connection. Then Dr. Stella mentioned he'd like to see me perform.

"I dance with my partner Angel at the MGM Park," I told him. "Would you like to come watch?"

Now, just weeks after that first coffee, Dr. Stella sat in the audience while Angel and I prepared for our cha-cha routine. As the music began and Angel guided me into our opening position, I felt the weight of convergence every thread of my story weaving together in this moment.

"You're different tonight," Angel murmured as we moved through our first sequence.

He was right. The presence of Dr. Stella in the audience charged the air with possibility. As we danced, I felt the culmination of everything I'd learned:

From Meatloaf: that presence matters more than perfection From Angel: that trust isn't weakness but strength
From my journey: that every challenge had been preparation

The music swirled around us as we moved through the routine. Each step felt weighted with significance. In the audience, Dr. Stella watched, and with every turn, every connection of hands, I felt the electricity building.

As we moved into our final combination a series of spins that required absolute trust I caught Dr. Stella's eyes. The connection was instantaneous, undeniable, as if the universe itself was holding its breath.

The music reached its crescendo. We hit our final pose. The applause erupted around us.

And then, in that moment that would change everything, Angel leaned close and whispered: "You've met your soulmate."

My carefully maintained composure cracked. My palms grew damp in Angel's grip. The truth of his words reverberated through every cell of my body the same body that had always known truth before my mind could catch up.

"Thank you," I whispered to Angel, my voice thick with emotion, "for preparing me."

As I walked off the dance floor toward Dr. Stella, time seemed to slow. He stood as I approached, and I saw in his eyes not just attraction but recognition of the journey that had shaped me, of the woman I'd become through every challenge.

"Would you like to go for a walk?" he asked, his voice gentle but certain.

He walked me to my car in comfortable silence, the desert air carrying promises of what was to come and our first real date took us to a quiet park, where we strolled along winding paths as the sun began its descent toward the mountains.

When he reached for my hand, I didn't hesitate. The same hands that had once trembled with fear at the thought of following now intertwined with his naturally, as if they'd always belonged together. We walked like that, fingers interlaced, hearts opening with each step.

Then, in a moment I'll never forget, Dr. Stella suddenly stopped. Right there in the middle of the path, with golden sunset light filtering through the trees, he dropped to his knees.

"Thank you, God," he said, his voice filled with such reverence that tears immediately sprang to my eyes.

I stood there, holding his hand as he knelt, and felt the enormity of what was beginning. This wasn't just attraction or compatibility. This was divine orchestration every injury, every setback, every moment of learning to trust had led to this sacred recognition.

As he rose and pulled me into an embrace, I understood that the dance I'd been learning my whole life had just begun its most important movement. The solo years had taught me strength. The partnered dances with Angel had taught me trust. Now, with Dr. Stella, I was ready for the ultimate dance one that would require everything I'd learned and more.

Vegas had called me back not to reclaim my past but to claim my future. Meatloaf had shown me how to be real. Angel had taught me how to trust. And now, hand in hand with Dr. Stella, I was stepping into the most sacred choreography of all.

The stage lights had dimmed on one chapter of my life, but a new spotlight was warming, illuminating not just me, but us. Two souls who had been divinely prepared for this moment, this recognition, this dance that would last a lifetime.

As we walked back through the park, hands still intertwined, hearts beating in synchronized rhythm, I knew with absolute certainty:

The music wasn't ending it was just beginning. The performance wasn't over it was transforming. The dance wasn't finished, the duet was beginning.

Every stumble had prepared me for this sure step. Every fall had taught me how to rise into love. Every solo had sculpted me for this sacred duet.

And now, as the desert stars began to emerge in the darkening sky, witnessing the birth of something eternal, I understood the greatest truth of all:

Sometimes God knocks us down not to end our dance, but to prepare us for the one that truly matters. Sometimes we have to learn to follow before we can dance as equals. Sometimes the longest journey leads us exactly where we were always meant to be home, in the arms of the one who sees us, knows us, and loves us completely.

The next dance was beginning. And it would be the most beautiful one yet.

As I explained at the beginning of our journey, the Lipstick, Lashes, and God framework offers a practical approach to authentic living. Now, having walked through my story, you can see how these three elements courage to be seen, perspective to find wisdom in challenges, and connection to divine guidance work together in real life.

As you move through your own dance of life, your own combination of lipstick, lashes, and God, know that every step, every stumble, every moment of grace is weaving you into the person you were created to be. The choreography may not make sense in the moment, but seen from above, it forms a pattern of exquisite beauty, your unique contribution to the great dance of love that moves the universe itself.

REVIVING THE SPIRIT

Reminders

Surrender is your gateway to freedom: Just as learning to follow in dance opened up new dimensions of movement, surrendering control in life opens pathways to unexpected blessings. What feels like giving up is often the beginning of receiving what you truly need. Trust that letting go of how you think things should unfold creates space for how they're meant to unfold.

Divine orchestration works through ordinary moments: God speaks through coffee invitations, chance encounters, and gentle nudges from friends. Pay attention to the seemingly small moments, they often carry the biggest transformations. The sacred rarely arrives with fanfare; it usually whispers through everyday circumstances.

Find presence through practice: Meatloaf valued my ability to stay present on stage and adapt to unexpected changes without losing my center. This presence didn't happen by accident it came through the daily practice of connecting to my body. Develop your own daily rituals that ground you in the present moment, whether through movement, breath, or mindful attention.

STEPS

Lipstick: Practice saying "Show up as you are" to yourself each morning. Like my ballet teacher's advice before the Meatloaf audition, give yourself permission to be authentic rather than perfect. Whether facing a challenge, opportunity, or ordinary day, choose presence over performance.

Lashes: Identify one area where you're "fighting the lead" resisting life's natural flow. Maybe it's a career transition, a geographical move, or a dynamic relationship. Ask yourself: "What would happen if I trusted instead of controlled?" See resistance as an invitation to discover a new kind of strength through surrender.

God: Create a daily surrender practice. Each evening, place your hands on your heart and say: "I release my plan and open to divine possibilities." Notice what shifts when you consciously choose trust over control, faith over fear, surrender over force.

PRAYER

For Divine Surrender

God of Divine Timing,

Thank You for teaching me that surrender
is the doorway to my greatest victories.
Grant me courage to trust the unknown path,
To follow when I want to control.

Help me recognize when I'm fighting Your lead,
Transform my resistance into trust,
My need for control into sacred surrender,
My fear into faith. Teach me that presence matters
more than perfection,
That following requires its own strength,
That letting go creates space
For divine possibility to enter. When challenges
arrive, help me see preparation.
When control calls, teach me to be still.

With ease please,
Guide me into Your divine flow,
Where surrender becomes strength,
Where trust becomes freedom.

I release. I trust. I follow.
Amen.

DANCING WITH DIVINE PURPOSE

My Dear Friend,

As our three-part journey from Preparation through Performance to Purpose comes to completion, I find myself filled with gratitude for the divine choreography that has shaped my life and for the sacred privilege of connecting my story with yours.

What began as my personal narrative of physical challenges, professional achievements, and spiritual surrender has become a bridge between us a conversation about how our perceived limitations often contain our greatest gifts, how apparent setbacks frequently redirect us toward authentic purpose, and how surrender ultimately leads to freedom.

I've shared how I got knocked out so I could wake up, how that backstage concussion wasn't just an injury but divine intervention aligning me with my true calling. Perhaps you've experienced similar moments when the universe used dramatic measures because you missed the subtler cues. Our stories may look different, but the divine language speaking through them is remarkably similar.

Throughout my dance career, I perfected the art of precision while believing success meant mastering external choreography. Meanwhile, the most important dance was happening within the sacred movement between body, mind, and spirit, guiding me toward authentic purpose. What external performances are you perfecting while your inner wisdom waits to be heard?

My scoliosis wasn't a barrier to dance but my unique signature. My wobbles weren't failures but information. My concussion wasn't my ending but the beginning of something greater. Your challenges carry similar gifts; they are not random obstacles but purposeful redirections, tailored specifically for your journey.

Throughout this journey, we've explored how the three elements of Lipstick, Lashes, and God dance together in creating transformation. The courage to express your truth boldly, the perspective to recognize divine purpose in all circumstances, and the connection to wisdom both within and beyond yourself these aren't just concepts to understand but lived practices to embody as you create your own sacred choreography. The wisdom I discovered and now share with you is this: Your purpose isn't something to find "out there" through perfect performance or others' approval. It's already within you, waiting to be uncovered as you honor your body's wisdom, listen for guidance in unexpected places, and align with what feels deeply true, even when it defies expectations.

Reviving Your Spirit

When your spirit feels depleted, when you've pushed too hard, listened too little, or lost connection with what truly matters, remember that revival isn't found in accomplishing more but in returning to your essence. As I discovered in the temples of Tokyo and the quiet moments backstage, divine presence surrounds you, waiting to be recognized.

Revival begins with honesty, the kind of raw prayer I offered during the Nativity scene when I admitted I wasn't happy despite "having it all." It continues with stillness, creating space to hear what your body, heart, and spirit have been trying to tell you. And it culminates in surrender, releasing your grip on how you think things should unfold and opening to how they are actually meant to unfold.

Your spirit revives when you stop treating your body as a machine to be conquered and start honoring it as a vessel of wisdom. It awakens when you transform "wobbles" into information rather than failure. It flourishes when you recognize divine messages in unexpected places, whether in a stranger's kindness, a timely email, that teaches you comfort matters.

The Courage to Move Forward

Moving forward doesn't always mean charging ahead. Sometimes it means pausing long enough to hear the still, small voice beneath the noise. Sometimes it means taking a single authentic step rather than many impressive ones. Sometimes it means honoring your limits today so you can expand your capacity tomorrow.

The courage I needed to wear a back brace for five years is the same courage you'll need to embrace your own unique journey. The perseverance that helped me transform wobbles into information will serve you as you navigate your own balance challenges. The faith that carried me through concussion recovery is available to you in your moments of forced stillness.
True courage isn't fearlessness but faithful movement despite fear. It's showing up authentically even when your hand trembles. It's seeing purpose in difficult circumstances. It's connecting with the divine especially when you don't understand the choreography of your life.

When my dance teacher told me, "I believe in you," it changed everything. So let me be the voice that tells you now: I believe in you. I know you have the capacity to transform limitations into liberation. I know you have the ability to find divine purpose in everyday moments. I know your divine gifts are a unique contribution to this world.

Lipstick, Lashes, and God: A Universal Framework

Throughout this book, I've used the metaphor of "Lipstick, Lashes, and God" as a practical framework for living authentically. While these symbols originated in my personal experience with makeup and spirituality, their essence transcends the literal and speaks to universal human needs.

Lipstick represents courage, the willingness to be fully seen in your authentic truth. Whether you wear makeup or not, this is about showing up as who you truly are, not who others expect you to be. It's about expressing your words intentionally, embodying your purpose fully, and sharing your divine gifts with confidence.

Lashes symbolize perspective, the ability to see beauty in unexpected places and wisdom in challenges. Just as eyelashes frame our vision, our perspective frames how we interpret everything we experience. This isn't about mascara but about choosing how we see the world and ourselves, recognizing divine guidance in unlikely messengers.

God represents connection, with divine wisdom, with your authentic self, with others, and with the universe. However you understand the sacred, this connection isn't just reaching outward to something beyond; it invites us to also attune to the sacred wisdom that has been within you all along.

Remember to add "with ease, please" to your prayers. Remember that your limitations might be redirecting you toward your greatest gifts. Remember that your life, like mine, is a divine tapestry being woven with purpose and meaning, even when the pattern doesn't match what you expected.

As you complete your journey through these pages, remember that your own three-part journey continues. Your Preparation with all its stretching, strengthening, and shaping has divine purpose. Your Performance with its achievements, questions, and redirections is perfectly choreographed. And your Purpose emerges naturally when you finally surrender to the dance you were divinely designed to perform.

My prayer is that through these pages, you'll discover the extraordinary possibilities awaiting within your own story revealing the unique and purposeful dance you were divinely designed to perform.

With love and reverence for our connected journeys,
Gina

PRAYER OF DIVINE GRATITUDE

Divine Choreographer,
With overwhelming gratitude, I welcome this new day's dance. Thank You for gifting me the courage to shine boldly, Thank You for blessing me with eyes to see beauty everywhere, Thank You for surrounding me with Your loving presence.

I am grateful for:
Every step that teaches and expands me,
Every moment that reveals Your purpose,
Every experience that opens new doors,
Every season that prepares me for abundance.
Thank You for lifting me higher each day.
Thank You for transforming me through Your grace.
Thank You for seeing me as whole and perfect
Divinely designed, uniquely beautiful.
With deep appreciation, I choose:
Presence to savor each precious moment,
Trust in Your exquisite timing,
Authenticity to express my true gifts,
Faith in Your magnificent plan.
Thank You for guiding my every step.
Thank You for strengthening my foundation.
Thank You for expanding my capacity to love.
Thank You for illuminating my sacred purpose.
With ease, joy, and gratitude,
I surrender to my own unique choreography,
Knowing every movement flows in harmony with the perfect schedule
I am grateful.
I am blessed.
Thank You, thank You, thank You. Amen.

The Divine Design

Your Sacred Journey

Your body holds wisdom beyond intellectual understanding. What appears as limitation a curved spine, uneven legs, heightened sensitivity is actually your divine signature, uniquely crafted to shape your journey. These aren't flaws to overcome but sacred markings guiding you toward authentic expression. Trust that, as my grandmother said, "God doesn't make mistakes." What feels like a burden today may be tomorrow's blessing in disguise.

Pain often arrives bearing gifts we only recognize through time and perspective. When challenges knock you down, look upward for angels in unexpected forms: a teacher's belief, a song's lyrics, a father's encouragement. These divine messengers remind you that beyond today's struggles lie tomorrow's joys. The message isn't that suffering will disappear, but that you're never alone in it.

What others label as weakness, shyness, sensitivity, or vulnerability, may be your greatest strength simply awaiting the right channel of expression. The studio floor becomes holy ground, not because you become someone new there, but because you discover who you've been all along. Dance positions hold wisdom your body understands before your mind: plié teaches flexible strength, relevé teaches grounded reaching, pirouette teaches finding stillness within motion.

The mist obscuring your future isn't punishment but an invitation to develop faithful presence with what's directly before you. Sometimes the single visible step a dance major, a move across the country, a concussion that halts your career is enough to move forward. Divine guidance rarely arrives in expected packaging. The concussion that ended my Rockettes season became the catalyst for my greater purpose. What appears to be knocking you down may be lifting you toward your true calling.

True surrender isn't weakness but a different kind of strength, the courage to trust while remaining authentically yourself. When you "show up as you are" rather than striving for perfection, you create space for divine choreography. Social dance teaches that following isn't passive submission but sacred conversation requiring both yield and voice. Your body recognizes truth before your mind, whether in a lead's gentle pressure or the unexpected calm from a first embrace.

Your most powerful prayers aren't wrapped in spiritual language but spoken from honest recognition of where you truly stand. The divine responds when you finally admit something feels off, even when everything looks perfect from outside. Life unfolds in divinely sequenced steps, rarely following logical order. Trust that each step, even painful ones, prepares you for what comes next.

The sacred fire exists in many forms, in temples, churches, the passion fueling your art, the love connecting across distances. Spirituality isn't about finding the one correct container for divinity but about recognizing the flame burning in all places and within your own heart.

As you close this book, carry this truth: The divine design of your life, with all its curves, sensitivities, challenges, and redirections, has been choreographed with exquisite intention. Every wobble teaches balance. Every setback reveals purpose. Every limitation contains a gift. The light may show only one step at a time, but it will always illuminate exactly what you need for the journey to continue.

Your lipstick, your lashes, and your God await the next beautiful movement in your sacred dance.

Afterword

When Gina first approached me about writing this afterword, I was deeply honored. As Chair Emeritus of the Department of Theatre and Dance at the University at Buffalo, I've witnessed her remarkable journey from a determined undergraduate with scoliosis to the wise teacher she is today. I witnessed her evolution from a promising student to an accomplished performer.

What makes "Lipstick, Lashes, and God" extraordinary is how Gina connects her formal dance education to profound spiritual insights. In academic settings, we often focus on technique, choreography, and performance, the external manifestations of dance. Gina's journey illustrates how these elements are merely doorways to something deeper: a sacred relationship with movement that transcends the stage and informs every aspect of life.

Gina has taken these universal principles of dance education and illuminated their spiritual dimensions with remarkable clarity. The title brilliantly captures her essence: Lipstick representing the courage to show up fully, Lashes symbolizing perspective, and God acknowledging the divine presence weaving through every experience.

The core message of this book is one our world desperately needs: Sometimes the universe removes us from the life we've carefully constructed to reveal the life we're meant to live. Gina's "divine knockout" represents a pattern I've witnessed repeatedly what appears to be career disruption ultimately reveals a deeper calling.

In your hands, you hold more than a spiritual journey, you hold a roadmap for recognizing divine guidance in unexpected packages. As Gina would say, remember to add "with ease, please" to your deepest prayers, for the universe is indeed listening.

May you approach your own divine knockouts with courage and openness. May you discover, as Gina did, that sometimes falling is flying toward your truest purpose the divine choreography that has been within you all along.

Dream Big and Dance Often.

Tom Ralabate
Chair Emeritus, Department of Theatre and Dance, University at Buffalo

Chapter Summaries with Reflective Questions

Chapter 1: *Divine Choreography When the Body Reveals its Wisdom*

Summary: Your body's physical challenges aren't punishments but pathways to deeper understanding. Through my scoliosis journey and discovery of Simonson Dance Technique, I learned that listening to body wisdom, rather than fighting against limitations, leads to profound healing and purpose.

Reflective Question: What physical challenge or limitation in your life might actually be guiding you toward a deeper understanding of yourself or a unique gift you're meant to share?

Chapter 2: *Curves of Courage Finding Grace in the Unexpected*

Summary: What appears as imperfection may be sacred architecture. My scoliosis and back brace weren't obstacles to overcome but unique designs with divine purpose. True courage comes from embracing your "flaws" as signatures of your authentic self.

Reflective Question: What aspect of yourself that you've been trying to hide or fix might actually be your divine signature the very thing that makes your contribution to the world unique?

Chapter 3: *Angels in the Sky Finding Grace Through Pain*

Summary: Divine messengers appear in unexpected forms teachers, songs, even strangers on airplanes. My ankle injury taught me that pain often carries hidden gifts, and that looking up during our lowest moments reveals the angels already present in our lives.

Reflective Question: Who have been the "angels" in your life during difficult times, and what messages did they bring that you might not have recognized as divine guidance at the time?

Chapter 4: *The Sensitive Soul - Finding My Voice Through Movement*

Summary: Sensitivity isn't weakness but a spiritual gift of deep perception. What others labeled as shyness was actually heightened awareness. Finding your sacred language whether dance, art, or another form transforms overwhelming sensitivity into powerful expression.

Reflective Question: How might your sensitivity, introversion, or the traits others have told you to "overcome" actually be spiritual gifts waiting for the right channel of expression?

Chapter 5: *Dialing Into Truth Four Words That Changed Everything*

Summary: Simple words spoken with belief can redirect a life's trajectory. Miss Lisa's "I believe in you" transformed my decision to quit dance. Sometimes divine intervention comes through ordinary people speaking extraordinary truth at exactly the right moment.

Reflective Question: What words has someone spoken to you that changed your life's direction, and who in your life might need to hear you say "I believe in you" right now?

Chapter 6: *The Next Step Finding Faith in the Present*

Summary: When you can't see the entire staircase, faith in the next visible step is enough. My journey to college and dance major wasn't my whole future revealed but the exact next move that opened unexpected doors.

Reflective Question: What next single step is visible to you right now, even if you can't see the whole path, and what's preventing you from taking it with faith?

Chapter 7: *Divine GPS From Vegas Lights to Christmas Nights*

Summary: Life unfolds in divinely sequenced steps that rarely follow logical order. Each step even painful ones prepares you for what comes next. My path from Vegas to NYC to the Rockettes followed divine choreography, not human planning.

Reflective Question: Looking back at your life's seemingly random sequence of events, what divine pattern or purpose can you now see emerging that wasn't visible while you were living it?

> **Chapter 8:** *The Divine Knockout - Finding Purpose Beyond the Spotlight*

Summary: What knocks you down may be lifting you toward true calling. My concussion during the Rockettes wasn't career-ending but career-beginning, answering my prayer for purpose in the most unexpected way.

Reflective Question: What apparent setback or "knockout" in your life might actually be a divine response to your deeper prayers for purpose and meaning?

> **Chapter 9:** *Starting Over When Discomfort Leads to Divine Direction*

Summary: Discomfort isn't punishment but guidance. Being stripped of familiar identities and achievements brings you closest to discovering authentic purpose. My return from Italy to my parents' attic led to the breakthrough I needed.

Reflective Question: What current discomfort or "backward step" in your life might actually be preparing you for a divine redirection toward your true purpose?

Chapter 10: *The Island of Remembering - When God Removes You to Restore You*

Summary: Sometimes divine wisdom removes us from everything familiar to help us remember what truly matters. My time in Sardinia taught me that slowing down, receiving care, and being present are not luxuries but necessities for spiritual revival.

Reflective Question: When have you been "removed" from your normal life (through travel, illness, job loss, etc.), and what essential truths about yourself did that separation help you remember?

Chapter 11: *Sacred Fire Finding God in Unexpected Temples*

Summary: The sacred exists wherever you approach with an open heart. My experience in Japanese temples taught me that divine presence isn't confined to familiar religious structures but lives in every sincere seeking of connection.

Reflective Question: Where might you find sacred connection outside your usual spiritual practices, and what unexpected "temples" in your daily life might be inviting you into deeper communion with the divine?

Chapter 12: *Divine Surrender When Following Becomes Freedom*

Summary: True surrender isn't a weakness but strength the courage to trust while remaining fully yourself. Learning to follow in dance and life taught me that releasing control creates space for divine choreography far beyond what we could orchestrate alone.

Reflective Question: In what area of your life are you struggling to maintain control, and how might surrendering that control actually lead to greater freedom and authentic expression of who you're meant to be?

About the Author

Gina Pero delivers transformative keynotes and workshops that blend powerful strategy with practical communication tools audiences can implement immediately. Known for her unique ability to make complex concepts accessible, Gina captivates organizations with actionable insights on resilience, authentic leadership, and purpose-driven success.

Speaking Topics & Programs:

"Lipstick, Lashes, and God" Gina's signature keynote reveals how life's disruptions become doorways to your highest purpose. Drawing from her personal triumph over scoliosis and a career-altering brain injury, she provides tangible frameworks and communication strategies that audiences can apply the very next day. Participants walk away with:

Practical tools to transform limitations into signature strengths. Immediate techniques for making aligned decisions during uncertainty. Strategic approaches to recognize and leverage pivotal transitions

"Leading from the Inside Out" This executive program transforms how leaders communicate and strategize within their organizations. Gina delivers concrete, easy-to-implement methods that blend strategic excellence with authentic presence. Organizations consistently report enhanced team communication, measurable improvements in decision-making, and immediate performance gains.

"The High-Performance Holistic Leader" Perfect for conferences and corporate retreats, this workshop provides ready-to-use tools for sustainable success. Participants receive a practical toolkit for maintaining peak performance without sacrificing wellbeing, with implementation strategies they can start using before they even leave the room.

Speaker Credentials:

An ICF Master Certified Coach whose clients include dance companies, corporate executives, and creative organizations, Gina brings 25 years of professional experience to her speaking engagements. As Creative Director of the Las Vegas Holistic Center and author of multiple bestselling books, she combines strategic expertise with practical, accessible communication techniques.

Her work has been featured in Dance Informa Magazine, Holistic Fashionista, and My Vegas Magazine. Currently on faculty with Adrenaline and Revive Dance Companies, Gina regularly delivers pragmatic, results-oriented presentations to international audiences.

The Speaking Experience:

Gina customizes each presentation with practical, accessible tools specific to your audience's needs. Her engaging delivery style combines strategic frameworks with step-by-step implementation guides that participants can apply the very same day.

Whether addressing intimate executive gatherings or delivering mainstage keynotes at international conferences, Gina ensures every attendee leaves with concrete takeaways. Audiences consistently report that her presentations are "immediately useful," "surprisingly practical," and "the perfect blend of inspiration and application."

Book Gina For Your Next Event:
To bring Gina's strategic expertise and practical communication tools to your organization, conference, or retreat, visit ginapero.com/speaking. Limited speaking engagements are available annually.

Connect with me:
www.GinaPero.com
YouTube @GinaPeroAuthor
www.Lasvegasholisticcenter.com
Ginas Books & Podcast !

PODCAST: *Messenger of Love with Gina Pero*

Reflective Notes: *Dates*

www.ingramcontent.com/pod-product-compliance
Lightning Source LLC
Chambersburg PA
CBHW070637160426
43194CB00009B/1477